LINDSAY ANDERSON

D0171191

series edited and designed by Ian Cameron

Lindsay Anderson

Elizabeth Sussex

Praeger

BOOKS THAT MATTER

Published in the United States of America in
1970 by Frederick A. Praeger, Inc., Publishers
111 Fourth Avenue, New York, N.Y. 10003

Library of Congress Catalog Card Number:
70–108985

Produced by November Books Limited

Printed in England

'In my heart there was a kind of fighting that
would not let me sleep . . .'

Hamlet, *Act V, Scene ii.*

*The author wishes to thank the Education Depart-
ment of the British Film Institute, in particular
Paddy Whannel and Linda Johnston, for providing
vital facilities during the preparation of this book;
also Brenda Davies, Gillian Hartnoll and the
staff of the Information Department and Library
of the National Film Archive, and John and
Marlene Fletcher of Dateline Productions for
their practical help. Thanks are also due to David
Robinson for reading the manuscript and to
Lindsay Anderson for allowing himself to be
interviewed and providing the material on which
the book is based.*

*Stills and photographs by courtesy of Basic Films,
Contemporary Films, Film Contracts, Ford Motor
Company, National Film Archive, National
Industrial Fuel Efficiency Service, Paramount,
Rank Film Distributors, United Artists.*

*Frontispiece: Anderson directing Richard War-
wick in* If . . .

Contents

Fundamentals

In the spring of 1949 the editors of the independent film magazine *Sequence* – Peter Ericcson, Gavin Lambert and Lindsay Anderson – reported that they had been to see a Fleet Street advertising agent about their decision to include advertisements and expand their magazine.

'Snowballs in Hell,' the agent said. 'Pardon me, but you've about as much chance as snowballs in Hell.'

They stuck to their decision, got a few advertisements, carried on with *Sequence*. But in 1952, when rising costs continued to outpace a sevenfold increase in circulation (from 600 to 4000), the end came. Anderson and Karel Reisz were co-editors at the close. 'Snowballs in Hell' were mentioned again. 'It is economically impossible to produce an uncomprisingly specialist, and an uncompromisingly independent periodical for a readership as limited as this,' they wrote. 'We've tried: it can't be done.'

Anderson was already on familiar ground, testing out the practical limits to which an unwillingness to compromise could be carried. Although this particular battle is one that he has continued to fight out in public ever since, its implications are usually ignored. Otherwise he would be asked less often why he has made so few feature films. It would be recognised that whether he turns down offers or whether the studios turn him down, the fundamental conflict is the same. This is a conflict that Anderson's conception of his function as an artist demands. He must like Blake 'Create a System, or be enslav'd by another Man's.'

'Artists find it difficult to survive in large organisations,' he wrote in *Sequence* 3, 'especially in large organisations which exist for the purpose of making money. The usual method in the cinema, however, is that the artist works as the salaried employee of a large corporation. This is the Hollywood system; and the most extraordinary thing about it is that a handful of great films has actually emerged from it.'

This might go without saying, except that it is hardly ever said – even by people genuinely searching for an explanation for the unsatisfactory state of the British cinema. At a recent seminar at the British Film Institute, for instance, there was much debate about the reasons why British directors make the sort of films they do, why they so often begin in documentaries, why they favour literary adaptations and so forth. Almost everything was put as if it were a matter of choice on the part of the film-maker, as if the films that people wanted to make got made. Anderson was recognised as being unique, referred to as a genius. But because he worked in such a very personal way, it was decided, no general conclusions could be drawn from his experience. Nobody wondered why it needed a particular kind of contentious and assertive talent to win through at all. Nobody drew attention to the fact that *If . . .* couldn't find a British backer, and was financed by an American company.

Great films have always been more likely to emerge, against all commercial odds, from the American cinema than the British one. The reasons that Anderson gave for this in *Sequence* are things he has been fighting ever since: The influence of Class ('It is not a middle-class trait to examine oneself with the strictest objectivity, or to be able to represent higher or lower levels of society with sympathy and respect – limitations which account for the ultimate failure of even so exceptional an attempt as *Brief Encounter*.') The absence of emotion, penetration, passion ('The standard British formula for scenes of emotional tension: "When emotion threatens, make your characters talk about something else in a little, uncertain, high-pitched voice".') And, perhaps, the irresponsibility of critics ('With an air of cheerful self-sacrifice which can only with difficulty be differentiated from extreme insensibility they sit through miles of rubbish every year, exercising on it their various talents for facetiousness and chatty insult; when a serious film arrives they relegate it, as often as not, to the bottom of the column, or lard it with meaningless catch-phrases. Ask a critic to see again a film he has already written about and he will regard you as one deranged.')

One way to appear uncompromising is to start off by lashing into the industry that will one day employ you. Anderson has since claimed that the industry ignored his criticism, but he subsequently sensed no prejudice against him as a direct result of it. Why should the industry pay attention? Its laws are not Anderson's laws, and he can take them or leave them as he likes. So the conflict is finally inside himself: more than a refusal to compromise, a temperamental inability to do so. The whole thing is uncomfortably reflected in an interview with Sam Goldwyn in 1951.

Goldwyn looked at *Sequence* and said what a fine magazine it was. Then he told Anderson how to boost the circulation. 'Get a pretty girl on the cover. Look at this – just a horse. Who cares about horses? Get some pretty girls inside . . . cut these stories shorter . . . feature a gossip column.'

Anderson explained that this could mean ceasing to be *Sequence*, and argued for a little. 'Life is compromise,' concluded Goldwyn.

'But this, wrote Anderson (characteristically having the last word) 'is not universally true. There are lucky ones whose great hearts, shallow and commonplace as bedpans, beat in instinctive tune with the great heart of the public, who laugh as it likes to laugh, weep the sweet and easy tears that it likes to weep. Blessed with that divine confidence in the rightness (moral, aesthetic, commercial) of his own intuition, a great showman like Sam Goldwyn has no need to compromise. That I suppose, is the chief reason for his success.'

Lindsay Gordon Anderson was born in Bangalore, India, in 1923. On the side of his father who, like his grandfather, served as an officer in the British army in India, the background was military and Scottish. Anderson's mother was the daughter of an English wool merchant who had married a girl of Scottish extraction (a Bell), so that Anderson himself is three-quarters Scottish, a fact to which he attributes his moral intransigence as well as a sense of not belonging to the English theatre or English cinema as such. Apart from one of the Bell ancestors who was, he believes, 'a painter and a bit mad, a bit wild and a bit drunk,' the inheritance was not a particularly creative one.

He was educated in a conventionally upper middle-class manner at a preparatory school on the South Coast, a public school (Cheltenham College) and Oxford, where he read classics for a year while doing a pre-officer training for army service for which he had volunteered, but 'only because the country was at war'. After serving in the 60th Rifles and the Intelligence Corps, he returned to Wadham College to read English.

At school Anderson was interested in acting, play-reading and films 'on a strictly fan level'. (He loved going to the cinema, kept scrapbooks and bought *Film Weekly*.) At Oxford he appeared in an O.U.D.S. production, a couple of productions by Kenneth Tynan and a production by Guy Brenton (with whom he was later to make *Thursday's Children*.) But the

Still: 'Look at this – just a horse. Who cares about horses?' – the cover still from Sequence 11, *from* She Wore a Yellow Ribbon.

atmosphere of amateur dramatics at Oxford, which he describes as 'very pseudo-professional and very competitive in a rather unpleasant way' didn't appeal to him, and he didn't have very much to do with it.

Up to this time he had very little knowledge of foreign language cinema or of the classics of cinema which were difficult to see during the war, and weren't shown at Cheltenham, although he remembers seeing *Citizen Kane* there. It was a year or so after the war, when he saw *My Darling Clementine* at the Odeon, Leicester Square, that he got what he describes as his 'first real creative shock in the cinema'.

Sequence began as the magazine of the Oxford University Film Society. One issue (called the Film Society Magazine) had been published before Anderson returned to Oxford. A second issue (*Sequence* 1) appeared after Anderson was at Oxford (in December 1946), under the editorship of Peter Ericcson and John Boud, who probably invented the title. To this Anderson, who had been in Paris, contributed an article on French films which he describes as 'a very superficial and ignorant piece, but my first essay at this kind of thing'.

Sequence 2 (Winter 1947) had a new format, and represented the first number of what the magazine became. It was edited by Anderson, Ericcson and Penelope Houston, and a still from *My Darling Clementine* appeared on the front cover. Ericcson, who shared Anderson's enthusiasm, wrote a long article about John Ford. Anderson's schoolfriend Gavin Lambert, who was then in London, was invited to contribute an article on British films.

'From the beginning,' says Anderson, '*Sequence* was rather in reaction against what we felt to be an inflated estimation of British films, which took place in a patriotic way at the end of the war when there was a lot of big film-making activity among people like Michael Powell and David Lean at Pinewood. From the first, we drew attention to the lively and dynamic film-making in America, as well as concentrating on, and discovering for ourselves, continental film-makers and film-makers of the past.'

The magazine continued in London from 1948, the majority of the later issues being co-edited by Gavin Lambert (who was writing scripts for advertisement films), Ericcson (who was working at the Foreign Office) and Anderson (the only editor who worked on it from start to finish). The editors wrote most of the copy, using pseudonyms like Alberta Marlow (the character played by Mary Astor in *The Maltese Falcon*) and Adam Helmer (from *Drums Along The Mohawk*) to give the impression of a larger number of contributors.

The last issue (New Year 1952) was co-edited by Anderson and Karel Reisz, who first met when an accidental double booking was made for them to look at films in the National Film Archive at Aston Clinton. Reisz, who was writing his book on film editing at the time, had come to see Greta Garbo in *Mata Hari*. Anderson was viewing *The Lodger* for a *Sequence* article on Hitchcock. They shared the movieola, watching both films (and coming back to London on the Green Line bus) together.

Sequence's line was that 'an ounce of truly – (personally –) felt enjoyment, or disapproval, is worth a ton of noncommittal guff.' Attitudes and ideals came over with some force, particularly from Anderson for whom integrity has always been a matter of committing and exposing himself. In fact there could be no better introduction to him than his own writing, which has all the personal qualities – the directness, the involvement, the feeling for 'poetry' – that he aims for in his films. In *Sequence* and in his early writing for *Sight and Sound*, he formulated principles that underlie everything he has since done in the cinema.

'The first duty of the artist,' he wrote in 'Angles of Approach' in *Sequence* 2, 'is not to interpret, nor to propagandize but to create. And to appreciate that a genuinely creative work of art involves the willingness to jettison our own prejudices and viewpoints, and accept those of the artist. If you expect all films about children at school to be realistic in style and psychological or sociological in approach, you will not be able to get much enjoyment from a fantastic, satirical masterpiece like *Zéro de Conduite*. If you have forgotten that poetry, visual as well as verbal, is its own justification,

Stills: Above – Ivor Novello in the still from The Lodger *used in* Sequence 9 *and Malcolm McDowell in* If . . . Right – Hattie Jacques, Jill Bennett *and Anderson in* The Pleasure Garden.

you will call *L'Atalante* sordid and obscure and join the critic of *The Times* in condemning *My Darling Clementine* to "the graveyard of mediocrity".'

Anderson, even in those days, couldn't help speaking from the position of the artist. His need to feel involved in what the serious film-maker was doing, made his reviewing perhaps more arrogant than most, even by *Sequence* standards. And as a film-maker he has always demanded absolute allegiance, not certainly from the audience, but from the people who work with him. 'The enemies are time – and anyone on the unit whose enthusiasm, energy, loyalty are less than total,' he wrote in *The Observer* about shooting *If . . .* 'Your demands are impossible: but how can they be less ? To make a film is to create a world.'

Perhaps because he is a perfectionist, creation for Anderson is always a battle; his often savage sense of humour has probably had a good deal

to do with his survival. Back in 1952 in James Broughton's fantasy *The Pleasure Garden*, you find him parodying something very like his own predicament. In this film, on which he was producer, he played the part of an unkempt and angry sculptor obsessed by his art.

'Is it beautiful ? Is it beautiful enough ? How can I make it more real ?' Grimacing horribly, he seizes his *oeuvre* from its pedestal and breaks it on the ground. 'Art is a hard mistress. Art is real. Can I ever·make anything I really feel ?' he asks, lying on a nude statue and slapping its thigh. 'A work of art has got to be alive,' he

muses, not noticing the girl who wants to be a masterpiece, undressing on a nearby plinth. His reaction on finally seeing her (and before carrying her off into the shrubbery) is 'How can I make her more real?'

Anderson's work is based on the assumption that 'art is real', and that cinematic art is 'poetry'. I shall be using the word 'poetry' so frequently in connection with Anderson's films, and his appreciation of the films of others, that some kind of definition is needed at the outset. What is meant by 'poetry' in these pages is a fusion between style and content, between the thing said and the way of saying it, that makes the two inseparable and at the same time creates something new. His poetry begins with realism, with images drawn from the everyday, that are also so charged with the artist's particular vision that they acquire a deeper meaning, intensifying reality and becoming in themselves an experience.

'Probably all my work,' said Anderson in 1968, 'even when it has been very realistic, has struggled for a poetic quality – for larger implications than the surface realities may suggest. I think the most important challenge is to get beyond pure naturalism into poetry. Same people call this fantasy, but these terms are dangerous because words always mean different things to different people. I would call *If . . .* a realistic film – not completely naturalistic, but trying to penetrate the reality of its particular world. I think Brecht said that realism didn't show what things really "look like" but how they really are.'

In the early years Anderson had little time for documentary – an attitude often thought to be contradicted by his own subsequent career. But both the critical attitude and his approach to documentary are consistent with the view he always held that superficial realism is not enough.

'The so-called "Documentary approach" has no doubt its very considerable virtues,' he wrote in a review of Rossellini's *Paisa*. 'It makes for realism, for authenticity of atmosphere, for sincere if unpolished acting. But to the extent that it inhibits the artist (in this case the director) from imposing his ideas on his raw material, from exercising his right to shape and to exclude, it is not conducive to the making of masterpieces.'

In *Sequence* 3 he made his position in relation to the Grierson school quite plain. 'During the 'thirties,' he wrote, 'young people who were seriously interested in the cinema tended to go into documentaries, and since documentary-makers believed in the importance of their job and were on the whole given a great deal of freedom, the results were very good. But today things are not the same. Fewer of us are any longer able to summon up that ardent, proselytizing enthusiasm for social-democracy which was the inspiration of the documentary movement.'

He then quoted Grierson writing to the effect that the origins of the British documentary movement 'lay in sociological rather than aesthetic aims' and suggesting 'that the individual life is no longer capable of cross-sectioning reality . . . that its particular belly-aches are of no consequence in a world which complex and impersonal forces command.'

'Against this attitude,' asserted Anderson, 'most (though not all) of us have reacted, and have come to realise more and more that the particular belly-aches of the individual life remain of the extremest importance, that they affect society as much as society influences them.'

In fact, Anderson always liked a certain kind of documentary. In *Sequence* he gave Flaherty's *Louisiana Story* a glowing notice, and picked Jennings' *Fires Were Started* as his personal choice among favourite films. His article 'Only Connect', written for *Sight and Sound* in 1954, remains one of the few authoritative assessments of Humphrey Jennings' work. It also gives a clear impression of the nature of Jennings' influence on Anderson's own film-making – an influence already apparent in his very early films and still permeating and enriching his style in the 'sixties. After pointing out that 'this unique and fascinating artist . . . made all his best films as official, sponsored propaganda during the second world war,'

Stills from Sequence: Fires Were Started (*right*) *and* They Were Expendable (*below*).

Anderson wrote: 'His subjects were thus, at least on the surface, the common ones; yet his manner of expression was always individual, and became more and more so. It was a style that bore the closest possible relationship to his theme – to that aspect of his subjects which his particular vision caused him consistently to stress. It was, that is to say, a poetic style.'

It was a very different style, but one as closely related to theme, that Anderson admired in Ford's *They Were Expendable*. 'When the material is genuine, and Ford's response to it a spontaneous one,' he wrote, 'his technique is characterised by its extreme simplicity . . . Certainly Ford's art is inspired by an optimistic faith in man's nature, a reverence for the human creature which is evident always in choice of subject and manner of treatment; but this is combined with a firm emphasis on discipline, an implicit stress on moral and social duties which may properly be described as classical, and which are matched by a sympathetic decorum of style. The poetry which, at their most intense, the films attain, approximates more closely to the Johnsonian "grandeur of generality" than to the romantic's glorification of the particular.'

Jennings and Ford are very dissimilar directors, but anyone familiar with Anderson's work will recognise from these descriptions alone, something of each in him. Both demonstrate qualities that were always of the utmost importance to him – qualities of courage, generosity, emotion, affirmation. His argument (which comes later) for moral commitment in film criticism was really a consolidation of attitudes plainly in evidence from the outset. All his own reviewing was committed: he and Gavin Lambert were unusual in conspicuously basing their criticism on the moral as well as the aesthetic impact of a picture.

'The climax of the film is a stylistic *tour de force*,' wrote Anderson of *Birth of a Nation* in *Sight and Sound* in 1953, 'but its amalgam of traditional, stagey melodramatics and hysterical racialism is extremely distasteful. The camera is tracking for the first (or the second) time in the history of the cinema; but where to? These hooded figures, whose actions we are so brilliantly being urged to approve; who are they, and what are they doing? Griffith is cross-cutting marvellously; but from what to what, and why? These questions are all part of film appreciation too.'

But if Anderson always wanted art to show a belief in humanity, a mistake that people make is to regard this as a simple notion. On the contrary a belief in humanity, intelligently held, becomes increasingly complex the harder you look at humans. It was a belief in humanity that led Blake to write 'Cruelty has a human Heart, / And Jealousy a Human Face; / Terror the Human Form Divine, / And Secrecy the Human Dress.'

To take the comparison with Blake a little further: most of Anderson's criticism and early films are Songs of Innocence (*Thursday's Children*) and Experience (*O Dreamland*). As with Blake the two apparently irreconcilable opposites are first presented separately, and later welded together in a single vision of the world. It would be pointless to try to force the comparison too far: Anderson's art is original and ultimately unlike anything else. But there are obvious resemblances between *If . . .* and Blake's *Marriage of Heaven and Hell*. 'Without Contraries is no progression. Attraction and Repulsion, Reason and Energy, Love and Hate, are necessary to Human Experience.'

By the time he made *Every Day Except Christmas* Anderson had laid the critical foundations on which all his subsequent work is built. From then on ideas and attitudes are developed, not through his writing, but in terms of theatre and cinema. His aim: 'not to interpret, nor to propagandize but to create.'

Early Films

In his first professional years, at least up to the appearance of *Thursday's Children* in 1954, Anderson was known as a critic, not as a filmmaker. Yet he had started to make films as early as 1948, largely by chance. In 1947 the Oxford University Film Society had played hosts to the Federation of Film Societies for their annual meeting. Among the society secretaries who came to Oxford for that summer weekend was Lois Sutcliffe, the wife of Desmond Sutcliffe, managing director of Richard Sutcliffe Ltd, a firm that made conveyor belts in Yorkshire. Lois Sutcliffe soon afterwards launched Anderson on his film career by deciding that he should make a picture about the Sutcliffe factory and its traditions. This was after she and her husband had approached two documentary film companies in London, and both had submitted scripts that were exactly the same. The Sutcliffes wanted not just a film about conveyors, but a film which was particular to Richard Sutcliffe Ltd, and which tried to get across something of the personality of the firm and of the people who worked for it.

Anderson made this film, *Meet The Pioneers*, with John Jones, the local schoolmaster, as his cameraman, and Edward Brendon (a friend of Gavin Lambert), who had been working as an assistant director on features at British National, as his general assistant. They bought a camera that Anderson had seen in the window of a Wardour Street store for £100. It was made to an Air Force specification, and proved extremely difficult to use, jamming all the time.

'I really knew nothing whatever about film making,' says Anderson. 'I learnt absolutely as I went along. I imagined that the editing of a film was simply the joining together of shots in an order that one already knew beforehand. So I only left myself with about two days in which to edit the film, which was a forty-minute picture. I probably edited it in four days. We had agreed to show it at a mining machinery exhibition two or three weeks after we'd finished shooting, so it had to be finished. It ended with me cutting for about 72 hours without stopping, and Desmond Sutcliffe sitting over us with a stop watch saying we had to make a cut every ten seconds or we'd miss the train to London. In London I'd made a booking to do the commentary, four reels in four hours, and of course the people at Merton Park thought I was completely mad.'

Anderson read the commentary himself, 'but I didn't know how you might edit commentary or lay it in different places. I spoke it to the picture, and that was it. And we put on the gramophone records at the same time. It was all extremely primitive and simple and absolutely common sense, since we didn't know anything about technique.'

Meet The Pioneers shows how conveyor belts

15

are used in coal mines, describes the history of the factory, and then shows how the belts are made. We see conveyors being used for the making of gas, for speeding up the packing of rug wool, for carrying limestone from a quarry in North Wales to await collection by the boats at sea. As a whole the film has very little shape, but there are qualities that you would expect to find in the first film of any director genuinely fascinated by the medium: an eye for composition, some splendid individual shots and a choice of music that complements the visual rhythm.

More particular to Anderson, however, is a sequence showing the lunch break at the conveyor factory. The commentary has just described how much the factory has expanded from its original row of cottages and single weaving shed. Now there are more than five hundred people to break for lunch. 'Some like to go home . . . Others prefer to eat their sandwiches in the traditional way, leaning up against the machines with a paper and a pot of tea . . .'

There are shots of people going outside, of the machines still and quiet; men eating sandwiches, relaxing in various parts of the factory, reading newspapers, talking, laughing. Outside men take their ease; a group of young people are chatting against a wall; two boys under a crane are silhouetted against the sky; a boy swings from a tree beside a stream; sunshine on the stacks; people beside a lake; boys swinging across the stream from a rope; laughter. The scene dissolves into a shot of the stockyards, from where the raw materials for making the conveyors are taken into the factory. And so we move back into the factory for the afternoon and the assembly of the largest conveyor of all, the Super Goliath.

To find this unstressed series of shots inserted here is like finding the beginning of Anderson's style.

The next film that he tried to make for Sutcliffes had to be abandoned because the camera was jamming so badly that the laboratories sent a telegram saying 'Suggest stop shooting.' For *Idlers That Work*, the next picture that actually materialised, Douglas Slocombe sold his camera to Sutcliffes. John Jones had moved away from Wakefield, and Anderson's cameraman (recommended by Slocombe) was George Levy, then a camera assistant at Ealing Studios. About a particular component of the conveyor (the idlers are the rollers under the belts), this shorter film is interesting only for the information that it provides, although it is more integrated in structure and more professional looking.

The third Sutcliffe film *Three Installations*, made in 1952, was the first of a succession of documentaries on which Walter Lassally collaborated as Anderson's cameraman. Lassally was one of a small group of sympathisers generated by the existence of *Sequence*: he was a friend of John Fletcher, who first put in an appearance helping to wrap up and distribute copies of *Sequence*, and of another young technician Derek York, who was film editor on *Three Installations*, and with whom Lassally had formed an amateur unit called Screencraft and made a film about squatters, *Smith Our Friend*.

The three installations are at an iron ore works, at a cement works and at a civil engineering project for the disposal of waste soil and slag. Lots of panning shots capture the sweep of huge conveyor installations, and an altogether more accomplished rhythm is taken up by orchestral music from Copland, Gillis and Khatchaturian and by a Conveyor Boogie for piano and drums. The final sequence dissolves backwards and forwards from the faces of the people at the design boards to the full-scale slag shifting operations outside, so that shots are continually being superimposed on each other. Although not particularly characteristic of Anderson, this is visually a good deal more ambitious than anything he had done before.

Wakefield Express was made for the occasion of the hundredth anniversary of the newspaper (not the fiftieth anniversary as stated in some reviews), and was originally intended to be a film showing how the paper is printed. Anderson was recommended for the job of directing it by the Sutcliffes and, with Walter Lassally, shot the picture on a budget of about £600. 'A friend was going to edit the film, but when he looked at the material, he said it wouldn't cut together,' says Anderson, 'so I had to edit it myself. This was the first time I had worked with John Fletcher. John came up to Wakefield and we recorded schoolchildren singing and local brass bands, and he also helped me edit the film.'

The Sutcliffe factory in Horbury had been the centre of Anderson's film-making until now. But in the very first film he placed it firmly in the semi-industrial West Riding landscape. The varied face of the industrial North of England is to be a significant setting for two later films, but Anderson uses it differently each time. These dingy streets of closely terraced brick houses that we ride past on carefree bus journeys in *Wakefield Express* become in *This Sporting Life* the claustrophobic expression of human inhibition and despair. In *The White Bus*, shot in the Manchester area, similar streets are part of an urban poetry of alternating moods and widening implications. By this time, the contrasts inherent in the North, between town and country, old customs and new developments, workaday beauty and hygienic conformism, are obviously reflecting a particular tension in Anderson's own temperament. But this is something that wouldn't have happened were it not that all along he had been using backgrounds primarily to show what

people are like. In all his films there is this direct link. The nature of their environment is written on the faces of the people; it is seen to have made them what they are.

Looking back at the industrial films, it is possible to detect already something of this feeling, but it could be there accidentally, simply as a result of using real locations and real people. In *Wakefield Express* there is no longer any doubt. Anderson is selecting the faces and the places. He is selecting and connecting and working out the basis of a style inseparable from an attitude towards people. So almost everything about the film is interesting because of the direction in which it points.

Wakefield Express has no recorded dialogue, just a commentary with music. The fact that Anderson made all his early films before actuality sound recording techniques had been developed meant that from the outset he had to use sound in a more consciously controlled way than seems necessary, for instance, to most television documentary-makers today. But if this sprang from necessity, it was also part of his deliberate purpose and aim. More and more his films are recognisably his by the way the

Frame: Wakefield Express.

17

sound comes in. *Wakefield Express* has before the credits a shot of a typewriter keyboard with typing noises, then the voices of children singing; these are the sounds that recur throughout the film – the sounds of work and of an innocent pleasure in community life.

The film opens with some sequences in Horbury, a place already full of personal associations for Anderson. The reporter, notebook in hand, talks to people in the main street, at doorways, in a lane. As he chats to the vicar, who is mowing his lawn, the voices of children singing break in again. There are conversations with a labourer digging a hole; a teacher outside the windows of the gymnasium where children dance; a bus driver who breeds budgerigars and is one of the committee organising the pageant for the coronation (band music for this, and some humorously observed interior shots with the budgerigars and the round mirror above the mantelpiece); a man who grows his own tobacco; a little old lady celebrating her ninety-eighth birthday in bed.

These sequences (as well as the ending of the film which includes a good deal about printing processes) are cut from the extract that is generally shown. But they have a freshness and immediacy, a kind of vigour that enhances the picture.

In Wakefield a hundred years ago they drove sheep through the cobbled streets. (A sketch takes us back to 1852.) Since it was founded, the *Express* has multiplied into a series of five related newspapers that cover the West Riding. Lassally's hand-held camera travels, sometimes a little shakily, into and out of town. Children are singing as we go on a bus journey along the country roads. We are introduced to the directors and editors of the *Express* in conference. Natural sounds come in behind the commentary for scenes in the printing room. A shot of a covered typewriter, held quite long,

suddenly makes the commentary unnecessary and introduces a sequence, rich in future associations, with the sports reporter at Wakefield Trinity Rugby League Football Club. Here, in striking contrast to *This Sporting Life*, all is sweetness and light, with children singing behind the practice game, and a few quiet shots in the shower room.

The travelling camera links a succession of newsworthy events: the Carnival at Pontefract; the unveiling of thirteen more names on the War Memorial at Sharlston; children giving a concert party for Dr Barnardos; the launching of a sea-going tanker at Selby; the welcome home for a channel swimmer. All these scenes are basic to Anderson's developing style: the child with her party dress and wreath of flowers yawning quietly in the Carnival float; the compassion for the woman whose face is shown in close-up at the War Memorial and, with the Last Post still sounding, the shot that conveys us on and away, past the grey cottages with all their memories on the hill; the close-ups of the children's linked hands, their shuffling feet, their unselfconscious faces as they sing; the music of 'Rule Britannia' joining the two scenes associated with the sea.

A quick succession of images of various recreations culminates in a shot of the woman director of Wakefield City Art Gallery, hanging a picture and suddenly smiling straight into the camera, involving us. The smile, with its vitality and expression, is central to the attitude of the whole film. Here are amusing, friendly people – individuals whose positive response to life and to each other springs from a sense of belonging to the community, of working and of enjoying leisure together.

During the processes of going to press, there is a gentleness akin to Jennings about the way the proof readers and compositors are shown at work, and in the shots of two elderly people placing their classified advertisements. This is the implicit respect for ordinary people and for work well done that is shown quite simply in Anderson's early films and becomes an increasingly complex element in his later work.

As the papers finally roll off the press, Anderson cross-cuts dramatically back to events and faces now familiar. There follows a typical relaxed scene, two men smiling; and on a misty Saturday morning the newsboy delivering the papers along a stately street. The

Frame: the woman at the War Memorial in Wakefield Express.

Wakefield Express is being displayed, bought, read, carried about. And back in Horbury's main street our reporter, notebook in hand, is out talking to people again. With reason, Anderson appended his initials to the end titles.

Anderson's last film for Sutcliffe's, *Trunk Conveyor*, made two years later in 1954, shows how a huge conveyor is built into a coal mine. Lassally was otherwise occupied at the time, and the cameraman was John Reid, who had worked before for the Coal Board. As the film was shot almost entirely in a pit, the Coal

Board safety lighting had to be used.

Trunk Conveyor has a stronger construction than any of Anderson's previous industrial films, and a lyricism that also points towards *Every Day Except Christmas* in its expression of a romantic, idealistic view of reality. Anderson's cinematic poetry has become more complex and less obviously idealistic the more he has grappled with what idealism really means. But it has always remained the product of a romantic, idealistic temperament. And people who misunderstand a film like *The White Bus* generally do so because they aren't looking for idealism.

The personal element is always present in *Trunk Conveyor*, with Anderson shouting 'O.K.' on the soundtrack before the credits, and an initial scene in which two fitters pause to light a cigarette before getting down to the job. Interestingly, there was a minor row over the inclusion of a shot of a golden syrup tin in which the men kept their grease. The tin immediately assumed tremendous importance for Anderson, who saw it as the kind of humanizing detail that he always wanted to get into his films. He cites the incident as typical of what happens whenever you try to put the truth on the screen.

The atmosphere of *Trunk Conveyor* is achieved largely by means of song sequences that alternate with technical or instructional passages. The first song, 'Sixteen Tons', comes in very near the beginning as a background to men working and coal moving on conveyors. The music from it is taken up again near the end, when coal first flows along the newly-built trunk conveyor.

The second is the collier's song, which comes in behind a landscape, a lorry moving along a winding road, miners emerging with blackened faces, groups of miners relaxing, smiling, talking. This is a pattern now becoming familiar: a firmer handling of the mood sequence first attempted in *Meet The Pioneers*. Passages or phrases from the music of this song recur at intervals throughout the film, providing a kind of emotional punctuation and bringing out the theme of people. With *Trunk Conveyor* as with *Every Day Except Christmas*, it is not technique that you first notice. It is people.

Thursday's Children and *O Dreamland* were both made in 1953. Anderson had by then shot *Wakefield Express* and all the Sutcliffe films except *Trunk Conveyor*; he had also written a book 'Making A Film' (published by Allen & Unwin in 1952), which describes the filming of Thorold Dickinson's *Secret People*. This was set up on the initiative of Dickinson, who felt with Ernest Lindgren that it was an interesting

Still: Thursday's Children.

way of following up Lindgren's 'Art of the Film' (by the same publisher).

Thursday's Children was Guy Brenton's idea. His job as an assistant with BBC Television had taken him to the Royal School for the Deaf in Margate, and he invited Anderson to co-direct the film he wanted to make about it. He and Anderson started to shoot the twenty-minute picture with their own money and money borrowed from friends. With Walter Lassally as cameraman they made up a unit of three, and where they had to synchronise the sound of the children learning to speak they used a portable tape recorder. Half-way through, World Wide Pictures stepped in and gave them enough money to finish the film. Richard Burton, the only actor they felt they could trust to speak the commentary without sounding like an actor, did it for nothing.

Anderson was not at this time a member of the cinema technicians' union. This had presented no problems in Yorkshire where he was in any case making films not intended for public distribution. But in London things were different. While the three of them were shooting *Thursday's Children*, nobody knew about it. When they came to edit the film at World Wide, however, a shop steward found out that Anderson wasn't a member of the union and told him to stop working on the picture. After an argument, he was allowed to stay in the cutting room but forbidden to touch the film.

'Of course when he went out of the room we just went on working, so it didn't really make any difference,' says Anderson. 'But it took two or three applications before I was in fact allowed to become a film-maker. The attitude of the union, or certain members of the union, which was very well expressed then and probably would be the same for a lot of them today, was that since I had a university degree I should be a schoolmaster.'

'When the film was finished,' said Anderson of *Thursday's Children* in a radio talk at the time, 'we hawked it about in the traditional way, and everyone was very moved, and all the distributors cried, but said of course it wasn't entertainment, and they were very sorry . . .'

After it won an Oscar *Thursday's Children* was shown on the Granada chain and in independent cinemas, but it never got a booking on a major circuit.

Guy Brenton had previously made only one ten-minute picture, *The Jason's Trip*. In later documentaries about epileptics, polio patients, faith healing at Lourdes, he was to look at pain and suffering in a direct, unflinching way. *Thursday's Children* differs from these in that it is not about the nature of suffering. It is about the joy of discovery, the joy of being alive.

Its striking quality is intimacy. It seems at first as if Anderson and Brenton simply got as close to the subject as they possibly could, and out of this proximity a style spontaneously grew. But the simplest effects are usually the hardest to achieve, and when style and content meet as perfectly as this, you can be sure that there was nothing fortuitous about it.

The children are unusually attractive, and so are their affectionate and unselfconscious relationships with each other and with their teachers. Lassally's camera never moves away from faces, constantly capturing in close-up the inspiring qualities of caring and of trying. None of this, however, really explains the achievement of demonstrating the nature of an enclosed and separate world. A comparison with *If* . . . is tempting and, I think, relevant. For *Thursday's Children*, too, was carefully constructed: the result of meticulous selection and rejection, an eye acutely sensitive to detail, a clear imagination.

Without imagination there could be no way of speaking for people whose experience you have never shared. What does it mean to be like the four-year-olds who arrive at this school

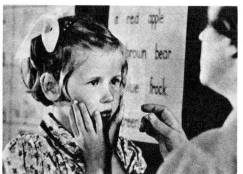

not knowing what a word is? 'Without words there can be no thoughts, only feelings with nothing to join them together,' says the commentary (which was mainly Anderson's responsibility). Immediately a tension is established between individual isolation and the need to connect, not just emotionally but intellectually. This theme that 'No man is an *Island*, entire of its self' runs through all Anderson's work.

Thursday's Children shows emotion and discipline working in harmony – the ideal at the heart of Anderson's most personal films. The

Stills: Thursday's Children.

picture as a whole has the kind of order that could be this way and no other. And every physical detail, every cut and every close-up, consolidates this sense of rightness, as the children work harder and harder to join their feelings together, to express themselves and communicate with each other, to be individuals who are also part of the whole.

What is sound? The children gradually learn what it looks like and feels like, by blowing small toys, by touching the vibrations made by their teachers' voice on the surface of a balloon, by feeling the sound of their own voices when the teacher holds her hand against their cheek. Then one of them, suddenly, almost accidentally, says 'bath'. Everything is cohering. The world is making sense. But this is only a single phrase in a poem, and other phrases follow quickly. There is harmony not just in single

shots and sequences, but in the way the whole thing fits together.

Towards the end of the picture we are told that 'only one out of every three children who are deaf can hope to achieve real speech'. We hear a pathetic attempt to articulate 'Little Black Sambo'. 'Thursday's child has far to go . . .' But these children, concludes the commentary, have 'a spirit in them that will make up for all the things they have to miss'. We leave them smiling and waving delightedly at the camera, at us. This is, of course, the kind of spirit with which Anderson always wanted his audience to identify.

While he was making *Thursday's Children* Anderson saw the amusement park called Dreamland. And shortly afterwards, with only one assistant, his friend John Fletcher (who was cameraman), he made the film *O Dreamland*. It was shown three years later in the first Free Cinema programme, but Anderson made it without any prospect of having it shown at all: 'I didn't mean to do anything with it. I just made it. What does a poet mean to do with a poem when he writes it, or what does a painter mean to do with a painting? You don't do anything with a ten-minute, 16 millimetre film. It's just there, that's all.'

O Dreamland is also set in an enclosed world. It also brings us very close to people – unattractive, dispirited-looking people, with whom the audience is never invited to identify. There is no commentary. The sound track consists of music and effects recorded on the spot and edited to heighten the effect of the harsh, derisive images. Obviously extremely personal, this is the first of Anderson's films that is open to more than one interpretation.

It begins outside the funfair, with four shots of a chauffeur polishing a very shiny Bentley in a back yard. On the fourth shot the camera pans away from the car to face the open gate of

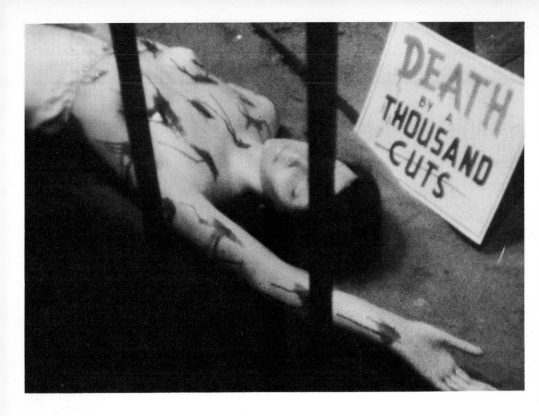

the yard. Outside people are passing on their way to Dreamland. In a fifth shot people are coming towards the camera, which is now in the street. A sixth shot shows the entrance to the amusement park; the camera pans down from the sign to the people going in. All this is shown to the accompaniment of brazenly cheerful canned music. On the next cut mocking mechanical laughter comes in on top; we are inside. Only the terrible laughter and a booming voice on the loudspeaker accompanies the next sequence of rigged-up atrocities: the representation of the electric chair in which the atom

spy Rosenberg was executed; torture through the ages; the burning of Joan of Arc at the stake; death by a thousand cuts – 'your children will love it'.

Already Anderson has established not only an attitude, but the basis of the editing technique that carries through to *If . . .* Something very like the first few shots occurs again and again in his films, as a statement, as an introduction to an area of experience, as a mood sequence, as the action out of which emotional reactions develop.

O Dreamland emerged in the context of what

Anderson later described as 'the blissful false dawn of the New Left'. In that context it could be taken quite simply as a particularly vehement protest against what passes for popular entertainment in the consumer society. The listless trippers are the oppressed, exploited victims of a spiritually nihilistic system. The car at the beginning, with its emphasis on affluence and materialism, shows this.

But like all Anderson's films *O Dreamland* contains far more of him than of any movement with which he was associated. He was always the complete individualist, which probably explains why his early work has dated so little. Looking at *O Dreamland* now you are less struck by its relevance to left wing ideas of the 'fifties than by its early avowal of the conflicting passions that led to the revolution in *If . . .* The contrast between *O Dreamland* and *Thursday's Children* is the first clear intimation of a conflict fundamental to Anderson's temperament and art. 'For man has closed himself up,' wrote Blake, 'till he sees all things through narrow chinks of his cavern.' And in the same vein: 'Energy is Eternal Delight'.

Can there be any doubt that Anderson hates, not just the entertainment, but the people – hates them for not fighting, for opting out of the battle that is life? Certainly there is very little evidence that affection guided his choice of glum faces, fat bottoms and feet shuffling among the litter. There is compassion for the little old woman in black sipping her cup of tea, for some of the children (perhaps), for the chained monkey, the pathetic caged animals. But for those who are not helpless there is only rage and scorn, with Frankie Laine's voice singing 'I believe' to emphasise the emptiness of their beliefs, the waste engendered by their passivity.

The film's pointed rhythm grows out of this anger: the camera panning round the crop of parked buses while the song says 'I believe for

every drop of rain that falls a flower blooms', or pointing upwards at tawdry swingboats in the sky as one pop number runs meaninglessly into another. The ruthless juxtaposition of dummies with people often uglier and scarcely less animated, of shabby images with shabbier aspirations, the brilliantly abrasive use of sound – all this minutely organised crudity forces us to react, to hate and by hating to feel alive.

Knowing what you are against is part of knowing what you are for. *O Dreamland* is a film with spirit in it. 'The worst sin towards our fellow creatures,' wrote Shaw, 'is not to hate them, but to be indifferent to them: That's the essence of inhumanity.' And in this way *O Dreamland* complements *Thursday's Children* as unequivocally as it contrasts with it.

Stills: 'Your children will love it'.

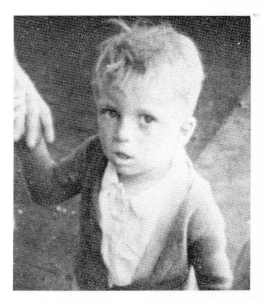

Anderson had edited *Three Installations* in the cutting room of the producer Leon Clore, and at that time Miriam Clore (Clore's future wife) had come from Israel to study film editing, and was observing the work of the director in the next cutting room to Anderson's. 'He was a very conventional and literally-minded unionist, and he wouldn't allow her to do anything, or to touch any of the film, and she got very bored,' says Anderson. 'So I said she could come into my cutting room and carry the cans about. She came and did little odd jobs, and was allowed to make some joins. And that was one of the ways in which I got to know Leon.'

The group of sponsored films that Anderson made after *Trunk Conveyor* were all produced by Leon Clore. Trailers for the Society for the Prevention of Cruelty to Children, a documentary about foot-and-mouth disease for the Ministry of Agriculture, a couple of very short films for the National Industrial Fuel Efficiency Service – they were all propaganda of one kind or another. Yet Anderson succeeded in putting enough of himself into most of them to make them interesting examples of a style now emerging with much clarity from a surprisingly small amount of actual footage.

The N.S.P.C.C. shorts were scripted and

directed by Anderson and photographed by Walter Lassally. *Green and Pleasant Land*, the most significant of them, consists of a series of images or tableaux: actuality shots of landscapes and of contented children singing 'And did those feet in ancient time . . .'; still photographs of the other, neglected ones, and of the appalling conditions in which they live.

The film dissolves from the faces of the children in the classroom to trees and panning shots round English landscapes, and as the hymn reaches the 'dark satanic mills' we are shown the other face of England, the filth, disorder, dirt and hunger that exists 'not only where the smoke of industry darkens the sky'. The images continue to dissolve one into the next, the camera slowly zooming into close-ups of the children who need help. 'What sort of men and women,' asks the commentary, 'can we expect these children to become?'

If . . . poses much the same question, and there are other resemblances between the two films. Both show situations rather than telling a story, and in both the development is similarly achieved by means of a cumulative, rather than linear, succession of short scenes. This is a uniquely cinematic way of creating drama – to pick up parallel threads of experience and make the tension grow out of their associations or inherent contradictions. *O Dreamland* did this, and this was the way that Jennings worked.

In *Henry*, a five-minute filmed drama for the N.S.P.C.C., the main part is played by a charmingly pensive small boy, spotted by Anderson among the schoolchildren who sang in *Green and Pleasant Land*. Anderson himself plays a subsidiary part as the N.S.P.C.C. officer who finally comes to the rescue. Shot entirely at night, this was the first film to use the new fast stock, Ilford H.P.S.

Henry is a straightforward narrative which includes a sequence at Piccadilly Circus that again uses a succession of shots for their effect

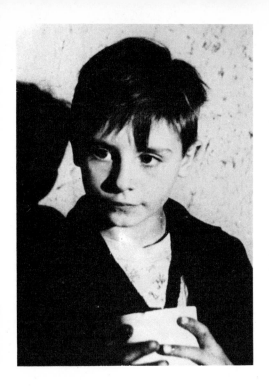

Frames: sponsored films. Opposite – Anderson in Energy First *(N.I.F.E.S.). Above – Henry (N.S.P.C.C.).*

he is caught by a guard and ticket collector at the railway station, he has also been offered a sweet by a stranger. A remarkably concise summary of the dangers that lie in wait for the innocent abroad, the film works largely because of the very direct appeal of the child's performance.

Children Upstairs, another brief filmed drama for the N.S.P.C.C., shows a young mother who has ceased to be able to cope. In their 'actuality . . . honesty, and . . . passionate pleading for what we have come to term the humane values' (I quote from Anderson's *Sequence* review of *Shoeshine*) these films strongly suggest the influence on their director of Italian neo-realism.

Foot and Mouth, also made in 1955, is a twenty-minute film showing the effects of foot-and-mouth disease among farm animals, and the action that must be taken to control an outbreak. Its description of this situation remains up-to-date, and the film is still widely booked for instructional purposes. It might seem the least likely place to look for poetry, and yet there is no other word for most of the first half of the film. This is Anderson and Lassally at their most evocative.

The setting is the fictitious but authentic Bury Farm 'somewhere in England, sometime in autumn . . .' There is from the outset a rooted sense of place and season. A few shots establish the outbreak of the disease: an aborted calf being carried from the cowshed; a still photograph of it lying on the grass, photographs of a dead lamb and a dead sheep; the notice 'Foot-and-Mouth Disease. Infected Place.'

Then the animals are slaughtered. There was at the time no possibility of filming an actual foot-and-mouth epidemic, and the whole impact of this sequence is achieved by means of associations, the interaction of sound and image. A man in black oilskins strides along a

in relation to each other. While his parents are having a row at night, the child steals some money and runs away from home. The film cuts sharply to Piccadilly Underground sign and jazzy music; it then cross-cuts backwards and forwards from shots of neon signs, crowds, shop windows, sex magazines, film posters, newspaper sellers, litter-strewn pavements to close-ups of Henry, taking everything in. In an amusement arcade the child sees a pickpocket at work and is given a cigarette. By the time field's edge; on the other side of the fence two farmers watch helplessly. We see close-ups of animals with the gun held to their heads; close-ups of people as the shots are fired. Each time a gun goes off, Anderson cuts to something else. This is at once a natural response to such an occurrence, and a dramatic way of heightening its impact by force of suggestion. There is no sentimentality. The commentary (spoken by Anderson) emphasises the waste in terms of the value of the livestock, nothing more.

Without seeing any carcasses, we get an equally vivid impression of the way the animals are destroyed. Men are carrying straw out to the bare fields, digging, dumping. A boy brushes the empty farmyard, and the single gunshots, slowly, deliberately, still go on. More and more infected herds from all over the area are being driven in for slaughter; long shots over the farm and across the fields alternate with close-ups of the victims. A wind gets up. Through the wire fences, the trees are swaying as the last dull shots explode in the far distance, behind the empty fields.

In the same year (1955) Anderson organised a season of John Ford's films at the National Film Theatre, and directed 'Secret Mission', the first of five episodes that he made for the television 'Robin Hood' series. This was his first experience of working in a film studio – 'the *inside* of the business that one has been criticising so confidently, from the *outside*, for a number of years,' he wrote in *Sight and Sound*. 'And it is fascinating to see one's own clichés come to life. Film-making *is* a compound of "Creative Elements"; also it *is* the director's medium – provided that the writer has given him the material to work with in the first place . . . In "Secret Mission", for instance, there was that scene where the Sheriff vainly attempts to persuade the outlaws to desert Robin, with the promise of a pardon. I liked that, and was even inspired to pinch a composition from

Wagonmaster to go into it. (I doubt, though, whether Ford would have recognised it. Those "nobility" close-ups are harder to get exactly right than you might suppose.)'

He found a good deal to learn on the technical side too. 'I had never before been able to indulge in the luxury of a dolly. My only tracking shots had been made from a conveyor belt; or by Walter Lassally sitting on a chair, hand-holding the camera, while I pushed. I was therefore ignorant of the acute geometrical problems which even a quite simple series of camera moves can present. This was something for which Arnheim, Spottiswoode and Eisenstein had left me unprepared. I learned the hard way, with much scribbling on the backs of envelopes.'

The 'Robin Hoods' which have been going out fairly regularly on television ever since as part of a series of over a hundred episodes, have nothing about them that would strike anyone as particular to Anderson. They are high-spirited and well-made to a routine formula. Anderson's enthusiasm is reflected, if anywhere, in the enjoyable performances of the players who, incidentally, include fellow director John Schlesinger (then an actor) appearing briefly as a baker in 'The Haunted Mill'. But Anderson

Photographs: commercials. Left – Kellogg's Cornflakes. Above – Lux, with Geraldine Chaplin.

had no control of casting, and was using what amounted to a stock company headed by Richard Greene as Robin Hood and Bernadette O'Farrell as Maid Marian.

Around this time Anderson also started to make television commercials, which he still intermittently directs as a way of earning bread and butter without making compromises in terms of more personal work. (The private income that he is generally known to have,

isn't large enough to keep him going for more than two or three months without finding work.) He makes the kind of commercials that involve actors rather than visual techniques: James Robertson Justice enunciating the name of Cracker Barrel Cheese; Bernard Miles downing a Mackeson's stout; John Sharp as a fat chef dementedly trying to wrap a turkey in too small a piece of tinfoil; families thriving on Kellogg's corn flakes. Anderson appears to enjoy this activity, which of course entails none of the usual battles. But if it isn't compromise, it's surely waste.

The Crusader

It was also in 1955 that Anderson undertook the supervision of the editing of Lorenza Mazzetti's *Together*. Lorenza Mazzetti was a young Italian who had come to London to study painting at the Slade School of Art, and had filmed two adaptations of stories by Kafka on 16 mm. When Anderson met her, she had shot *Together* (which shows the daily life of two deaf-mutes) in the East End of London, and was trying to edit it. 'She wasn't able by herself to put a fifty-minute film together. But such were the exigencies of the British Film Institute Fund, or the British Film Institute Production team, that they thought they could put Lorenza Mazzetti into a cellar in Denmark Street, and expect her to come up with an edited film. I saw the material – because she was very distressed about it – and I thought this *must* be finished. So I volunteered to take on the supervision of the completion of the film. Leon

Clore lent us a cutting room; John Fletcher helped us, and Walter Lassally did some extra shooting.'

About this time Karel Reisz and Tony Richardson were finishing their short *Momma Don't Allow*, which was one of the first productions of the British Film Institute Experimental Fund. Discussing with Anderson what they were going to do with these films, they got the idea of putting them together in a programme, and it was probably Karel Reisz who suggested showing them at the National Film Theatre where he was in charge of programme planning from 1952 to 1955. They decided that three films were needed. Nothing had ever been done with Anderson's *O Dreamland*, and with *Together* and *Momma Don't Allow* it made up a nicely balanced programme. Anderson thought of the name Free Cinema – 'a title that I had coined years before for an article that had been sent into *Sequence* by Alan Cooke (who has been working in television and who recently made his first feature film). He was in America then, and had written about American avant-garde shorts. I had rewritten this article to make it a bit more "important". I coined the phrase "Free Cinema" which I put into the last paragraph, and I called the article "Free Cinema". We always did this on *Sequence*; we were always rewriting people's things.'

The first Free Cinema programme was shown at the National Film Theatre in February, 1956, and gained a large amount of publicity, more perhaps for the idea than for the individual films. Only three of the six programmes consisted of films made in Britain; the others included Franju's *Le Sang des bêtes*, Rogosin's *On The Bowery*, Polanski's *Two Men and a Wardrobe*, Truffaut's *Les Mistons* and Chabrol's *Le Beau Serge*.

In the British programmes, eleven pictures were represented, five of them sponsored by the British Film Institute's Experimental Fund, and two by the Ford Motor Company. Eight of the eleven British films were made by a group of friends and collaborators – people who shared similar sympathies and who intuitively worked well together. Linking these pictures are the names of Walter Lassally and John Fletcher, who both helped with *Together*.

Lassally, Anderson's cameraman on *Wakefield Express* and *Every Day Except Christmas*, was also cameraman on *Momma Don't Allow*, on Karel Reisz's *We Are the Lambeth Boys* and on Robert Vas's *Refuge England*. Fletcher, who assisted on Anderson's *Wakefield Express*, *O Dreamland* and *Every Day Except Christmas*, was also cameraman and sound recordist on Claude Goretta and Alain Tanner's *Nice Time*, and editor and sound recordist on *Momma Don't Allow* and *We Are The Lambeth Boys*.

The feeling of working inside a group, with people to whom everything needn't be explained, made an unusually personal kind of film-making possible. For Anderson the experience was so important that he never seems to have relinquished the idea of bringing something of it into full-scale film-making within the commercial structure. It was this, for instance, that prompted him to ask the Czech cameraman Miroslav Ondricek to shoot *The White Bus* and later *If . . .* He saw Ondricek shooting Milos Forman's *A Blonde in Love* at a shoe factory outside Prague, and the whole way that they were working together reminded him of the Free Cinema days.

1956, the year of Suez and of Hungary, was a crucial point in British culture of the 'fifties.

It was the year that the English Stage Company produced John Osborne's *Look Back In Anger* at the Royal Court Theatre, as well as the year Free Cinema began; in politics it was the beginning of the New Left. The idea of Free Cinema was very much a part of all this. The idea (that is, the propaganda) and the films were never quite the same thing. This is even more obvious now than it was at the time. The propaganda, most of which bears the unmistakeable Anderson stamp, did two things.

Firstly it advocated the *Sequence* approach to film-making as an 'expressive and personal use of the medium'. The credo, for instance, ran as follows:

'No film can be too personal.

The image speaks. Sound amplifies and comments. Size is irrelevant. Perfection is not an aim. An attitude means a style. A style means an attitude.

Implicit in our attitude is a belief in freedom, in the importance of people and in the significance of the everyday.'

Secondly it related this to the contemporary situation in the industry, and to the kind of attitudes awakened by the New Left. From the start the films were presented as 'a challenge to orthodoxy'.

'In a climate as habitually conventional and free from excitement as that of the British cinema,' ran a later statement, 'almost any sign of vitality, or reaction against the norm, would be of note. But the lively continuance of Free Cinema as a movement is of particular significance. Like other youthful movements of the moment, in art, in literature, it reflects an increasing awareness of the relationship between art and society . . .

'The success of these shows and the interest in the movement has encouraged us to hope that here is an idea that may have raised a number of questions not merely to film-makers and enthusiasts, but to anyone seriously concerned with present day realities in our country.

'For instance: Why do we not use the cinema; and what are the implications of this neglect? Is it not strange that at a time when so much emphasis is being put on the ideals of community, this medium (above all potent in the service of such ideals) should be abandoned to irresponsible commerce? Why do so many thinking people not take a more active interest in an art so popular? And is it not time that artists whose convictions are humanist started to consider a little more seriously their relationship with their audience, the kind of use that can best be made of these mass media, so that their art be neither exclusive and snobbish, nor stereotyped and propagandist – but vital, illuminating, personal and refreshing?'

All this related to the films themselves only in the sense that they showed an awareness of contemporary working-class life. Due perhaps to the platform on which they were presented, they tend to be wrongly remembered as statements of social conscience.

'This programme is not put before you as an achievement, but as an aim,' ran the introduction to Free Cinema 3 (which included *Every Day Except Christmas*). 'We ask you to view it not as critics, not as a diversion, but in direct relation to a British cinema still obstinately class-bound; still rejecting the stimulus of contemporary life, as well as the responsibility to criticise; still reflecting a metropolitan Southern English culture which excludes the rich diversity of tradition and personality which is the whole of Britain.'

Films cannot normally be made unless there is some guarantee that they will be shown. It therefore was, and still is, the distributors and exhibitors who dictate the kind of pictures that are made. The Free Cinema argument was that the film-going public wanted something different, and rather more relevant to their own lives, than these middle-men were providing. The distributors and exhibitors were attacked on two counts: for wrongly assessing public demand; and for catering (as a result of the distribution system) only for a mass audience.

On the first count, the Free Cinema attitude radically affected the attitude of the British film industry a surprisingly short time later. Contemporary, allegedly controversial subjects, working-class settings, location shooting in the North of England, became the vogue. And not all the pictures that resulted were otherwise unremarkable. Karel Reisz' *Saturday Night and Sunday Morning* (the best of them before *This Sporting Life*) made expressive use of the medium in a way that sprang directly from the undiluted, uncompromised influence of Free Cinema.

As far as Anderson personally is concerned, the spirit of the last programme note (March 1959) has very obviously carried through all his subsequent career:

'In making these films, and presenting these programmes, we have tried to make a stand for independent, creative film-making in a world where the pressures of conformism and commercialism are becoming more powerful every day. We will not abandon these convictions, nor the attempt to put them into practice . . .

'Free Cinema is dead. Long live Free Cinema!'

Sometime during 1956 Anderson remembers sitting on one of the *Robin Hood* sets at Walton-on-Thames, correcting the proof of an article, which The Observer had invited him to write about its own exhibition commemorating sixty years of cinema. The exhibition was in his opinion 'the absolute sanctification of The Observer's kind of dilettante view of the cinema.' And the following Sunday his article didn't appear although, he says, he had told them what it would be like. 'I heard afterwards that the editor had read it, and been terribly angry, and cut it out of the paper.'

As a result Anderson took the nucleus of the piece and developed it into an article called 'Stand Up! Stand Up!', which appeared in *Sight and Sound* that autumn. By then it had become an argument for commitment in film criticism, with the Observer exhibition serving as an illustration of an attitude he deplored. 'Essentially,' the article ended, 'there is no such thing as uncommitted criticism, any more than there is such a thing as insignificant art. It is merely a question of the openness with which our commitments are stated. I do not believe that we should keep quiet about them.'

People tend not to forget this piece, perhaps because it was so passionate, or perhaps because it concerned so much else besides film criticism:

'We have had our social revolution: we have a fine system of social security: and our technological achievements are something to be proud of. How then to explain the prevalence of cynicism, the baffled idealism and the emotional fatigue? Why are so many young voices resentful and defeatist rather than pugnacious and affirming? . . .

'The young people who respond so unmistakeably to *Look Back In Anger* are responding to its outspoken attacks on certain venerable sacred cows, and also to its bitter impatience with the moral vacuum in which, they feel, public life, and cultural life, is today being conducted . . .'

Many of the young people who have responded so unmistakeably to *If* . . . would probably find a good deal to interest them in 'Stand Up! Stand Up!' In the context of Anderson's career, the article is also important in expressing the feeling that he had just prior to making *Every Day Except Christmas* – the feeling on which he based the publicity for the film.

'It is in the light of my belief in human values that I have endeavoured to make this film

Still: Every Day Except Christmas.

about Covent Garden market,' he said in what must be one of the most idealistic programme notes ever written. 'I hope it makes my commitment plain.' Elsewhere in the programme note is the famous statement: 'I want to make people – ordinary people, not just Top People – feel their dignity and their importance, so that they can act from these principles. Only on such principles can confident and healthy action be based.'

Every Day Except Christmas was made in the first place because Karel Reisz had taken a job with the Ford Motor Company, which involved supervising and making advertisement films. He did it on condition that he was allowed to produce a series of documentaries which were not based on advertising and didn't have to carry anything about the Ford Motor Company, and he asked Anderson to make the first film.

'We didn't know what it should be about,' Anderson recalls. 'It's always rather difficult when you're invited to do anything. I thought that, as a kind of anchor, we should perhaps put something to do with transport and Ford vehicles into it. The first idea I had was to do

with fishing and the landing of the catch and the transport of fish throughout Britain. Perhaps it was a subject that I always had a certain feeling for: the kind of epic and dynamic feeling there would be in long-distance lorry driving for instance. There was a project, probably about this time, to make a documentary for the BBC on long-distance lorry drivers. Norman Swallow practically commissioned me to do it, and then the BBC decided that they didn't make films by outside directors.'

When the idea of Covent Garden first came up, Anderson went there for two or three nights and stood around 'feeling extremely uninspired. They wanted me to do some more Robin Hood films, and I even said to Karel, would he mind if I did some more Robin Hood films? And Karel said "No, you've got to do this. You've just got to start".'

After making a very rough summary of what the film should contain, and becoming acquainted with the boys and one or two of the personalities who appear in it, Anderson started. Apart from a skeleton treatment that could be written on the back of an envelope, the film was improvised on the spot. Shooting was followed by about five months' work in the cutting room.

Just after he made it, Anderson described *Every Day Except Christmas* as 'a lyrical documentary – an attempt to bring poetry and humanity back into this kind of film-making, and to break with the technical-informational-travelogue tradition that in the past few years had made documentary synonymous with dullness and conformism.'

The last and most avowedly poetic of his documentaries of the 'fifties, this is the straightforward expression of a crusading spirit. The quality in his films that Anderson describes as poetic always starts with realism and always says something about his own ideals. But later, in *The White Bus*, *The Singing Lesson* and *If . . .*, it takes into account the relationship between these ideals and the fact of compromise. It more and more expresses the idealistic ambiguities of a generation that believes with Jimmy Porter that 'there aren't any good, brave causes left'.

By comparison, the attitude in *Every Day Except Christmas* is humane and patriotic in an uncomplicated way. The film was trying to revitalise that sense of community that seems to inspire the British people only in time of war. Using many of Jennings' methods Anderson succeeded in creating symbols of affirmation in the peace-time context where Jennings failed. But *Every Day Except Christmas* is a youthful film: the last of Anderson's Songs of Innocence and the last film he was ever to make in quite this optimistic spirit of unqualified delight.

The film works in the first place because of Anderson's remarkable talent for making people interesting. He dedicates it 'affectionately' to individuals in the market, 'to Alice and George and Bill and Sid and Alan and George and Derek and Bill and all the others . . .' And affection is the best word for the way in which he consistently shows them, implying both a relationship and a natural equality. These are people who work, not working-class people. Anderson shows himself to be more Scottish than English in his apparent unawareness of the existence of class. There is always room in his films for personal interpretation, and people who find class-consciousness in *Every Day Except Christmas* could be projecting it on to the film themselves.

The whole construction is a marvellous example of the artist 'imposing his ideas on his raw material . . . exercising his right to shape and to exclude'. Anderson excludes quite a lot. The porters in this film, for instance, belong to a different world from the people in *O Dreamland*. The fact that they might frequent a place like Dreamland in their spare time is irrelevant to what Anderson wants to tell us about them. *Every Day Except Christmas* is consistently idealistic. The more you analyse it, the more the detail adds up in this way. I shall try to describe something of the effect of the first few sequences.

At a market garden in Sussex, Brian and Dennis are loading the mushrooms that they take up to London every night. As the lorry pulls out it is almost midnight. On their radio the Light Programme is closing down: 'If you're working through the night, or if you have to be up, well, we hope it'll be a quiet, uneventful time for you. But if you're going to bed now, goodnight and sleep well.' The familiar roll of drums leads into the National Anthem and a prolonged tracking shot that carries us (with Brian and Dennis) out into country roads, through lit deserted towns, past residential suburbs, on through the night towards London.

Sound and image, working together, give a widely recognisable picture of Britain, the Britain that extends outwards from Big Ben and the Houses of Parliament and, at least for anybody British, they conjure up a host of associations that are both personal and communal. When the anthem ends the commentary takes over behind that continuing, extraordinarily fervid tracking shot: 'All through the night, through cities and country towns and down the long arterial roads, the lorries are coming to London, with apples from Kent and Evesham, potatoes from Norfolk, oranges and lemons from the Western ports.'

The associations are spreading wider now, to sunlit orchards and school geography lessons and the consciousness that Britain is an island.

Stills: Every Day Except Christmas.

The difference between this and a film like *Night Mail* is the tension between sound and image out of which ideas grow. Sound and image each carry different implications, and never just run parallel to each other. The rhythm is not inherent in either taken separately; it exists only as an amalgam of the two.

The tracking shot ends. 'All these roads lead to London.' There is a still shot of the market, lamplit, bare like an Ozu set, silent until the sound of whistling, and then the noises of barrows and footsteps, start to creep in behind. Gradually people walk into this still market place, and through it. Activity builds up slowly at the back. Two porters come straight towards the camera in the centre.

Again the rhythm changes. The next phase is a succession of short takes: aspects of work starting on the displays, gratings being removed, boxes, sacks, crates being unloaded, movement in the surrounding streets. The camera is still, but there is more and more activity inside each frame. 'All through the market displays are starting to grow. Some people believe in getting right down to it. Others prefer to start with a cup of tea and a chat, the cheerful way.' Sid, a leading character, waiting for his big load – the mushrooms from Sussex – has tea and a chat.

After the mushroom lorry pulls in, the camera takes up the activity. At first it moves slowly, following the people. Then as the action widens out over the market, it makes larger sweeping movements, and the sound builds up: whistling, singing, banging of crates and trolleys. The rumbling of a heavy flower barrow turns to music. In another succession of short takes, the flower boxes are opened: chrysanthemums, daffodils, lilies, tulips, carnations. The music accelerates as the flowers are raised on the stands.

Sound is always integral to the shape of the film. The scene when the boys are chatting over their cup of tea uses a direct recording, taped on the spot. But most of the soundtrack is a creative assembly of noises recorded separately: sounds of the market and of the busy streets, snatches of conversation and of song, the music of a street band and Daniel Paris's score, most of which grew out of variations on two themes provided by the street band. The aural picture is consequently as perfect an example of the artist shaping and selecting as the visual one. The porters' whistling and the songs they sing build up the same sense of satisfaction at work well done as the skill with which they handle the flowers or polish the faces of the apples. And so the work itself makes all the patterns, visual and aural, that continue to unfold endlessly out of each other, referring backwards and forwards, creating a larger harmony out of an infinite number of minor inflections and variations.

At half-past four in the morning, the displays have been completed and the boys go off for a break. There is a shot of the empty market, a cat silently padding through between the rows of flowers; then a café sign. The camera pans down to show the boys entering the café. This is like the beginning of *O Dreamland*, and the way Anderson always changes key.

Music blaring from the radio covers up the conversation in the café. 'Not everyone you find in Albert's works in the market,' says the commentary. 'Some of them – you wonder where they come from. They come in at two or three in the morning, have a bite to eat, talk for a bit. Then they go. And you wonder where.'

A middle-aged man combs his wavy hair with a kind of sad bravado. A woman with a face that was once beautiful talks animatedly and nibbles at a sandwich. A man with a lined forehead and unhappy eyes gesticulates with a very dirty thumb and suddenly stares blankly into the camera. The music stops. There is a shot of a cat, arched on the top of a pile of boxes,

Stills: the café scene.

then a display of flowers, then a tired, dejected woman in the café. The music that we have come to associate with flowers and momentary repose comes in. The images get sleepier: a man nods over the table; a boy rests his head on his arm. The camera pans very slowly along a massed display of tulips and then, in a series of shots that dissolve into each other, along more and more flowers.

'This is the world:', they quoted Dylan Thomas on the Free Cinema programme, 'the

lying likeness of /Our strips of stuff that tatter as we move /Loving and being loth; /The dream that kicks the buried from their sack /And lets their trash be honoured as the quick. /This is the world. Have faith.' This café scene is the first strong intimation of something that later becomes a characteristic element in Anderson's work: the ambiguity that makes us ask questions. What kind of rest is there for these other people, who like company and who perhaps like flowers? What are our feelings towards them, and Anderson's feelings? The scene is a recognition that there are no simple answers. It is as critical or compassionate towards these people as we ourselves feel.

Every Day Except Christmas carries us far into the morning: the arrival of the street band; the early bustle to get the vegetables into the shops by nine; the lull that occurs around ten or ten-thirty when George can put his empty boxes away and Alice, the last of the women porters, can get her weight off her feet. Then the old ladies who sell their flowers in the London streets arrive. In a splendidly caught snatch of actual dialogue we hear them explaining how things aren't what they were. 'When Jenny started selling flowers on street corners,' the commentary tells us, 'Victoria was

Queen, and every gentleman wore a buttonhole.'

Tradition is a large part of Covent Garden and an important element in all Anderson's work. *Every Day Except Christmas* is about a healthy tradition, the kind of tradition that gives people a sense of belonging, a common purpose in life. Appropriately the film ends with a succession of cheerful smiles, and a laughing close-up of one of the young porters looking directly into the camera.

A documentary record of the Campaign for Nuclear Disarmament's first Easter march to the atomic weapons factory at Aldermaston in 1958, *March to Aldermaston* was a project initiated not by Free Cinema, but by Derrick Knight and a committee comprising Allan Forbes, Kurt Lewenhack, Charles Cooper, Christopher Brunel, Lewis McLeod, Elizabeth Russell, Eda Segal, Derek York, Karel Reisz and Anderson.

During the four days of the march slightly over three hours of film was shot with a varied assortment of cameras (only one of which was synchronised for sound) on odd ends of film stock donated by people like Leon Clore or collected from the junk rooms of Pinewood Studios. The directors, not all of whom were present for all four days, included Derrick Knight (who was producer), Stephen Peet, Derek York, Kurt Lewenhack, Reisz and Anderson. Manning the cameras were Brian Probyn, Lewis McLeod, Wolfgang Suschitzky, Peter Jessop, Bill Smeaton-Russell, Allan Forbes, Derek York.

Anderson had become involved as a result of his connections with the New Left and *Universities and Left Review*, who supported the march. 'It rather brought into focus a lot of the new would-be radical, left-wing, youthful movement and feeling that there was at the time,' he says. From what is generally regarded as a hard-boiled industry, enormous numbers of film people turned up to work on it at all hours and, of course, for no pay, at every stage in the proceedings. Anderson took over the supervision of the editing, and worked in the cutting room with Mary Beale. Christopher Logue did some writing for the commentary, the final version of which was Anderson's; Richard Burton spoke it at Anderson's invitation.

The marchers, like many of the people involved in making the film, had little in common apart from their opposition to the manufacture and testing of H-bombs. They were of all ages, classes and political persuasions, just 'ordinary people' as the commentary said, who believed in living. There was consequently, on these marches, that feeling of being an individual with an individual point of view and yet belonging to a group, which is very much the spirit of an early Anderson film. Unfortunately, the material wasn't good enough to enable him to bring this out.

'My sympathies were with the Campaign without having thought it through to a very final political position,' he says. 'Certainly my moral sympathies were with the march. But even in the film, I think, is perhaps observable a certain back-pedalling on the militant and optimistic spirit, because my feeling was always that it was a sort of rather splendid, romantic, forlorn gesture. I mean, when the marchers pass those people standing at gates looking at them with the typical, unimaginative, phlegmatic smugness of the British working class, there is perhaps the same kind of confrontation there as you get in a more violent mood at the end of *If . . .*'

March to Aldermaston is of interest here for the way in which Anderson has imposed his own distinctive pattern on it: a pattern similar to that of *Every Day Except Christmas*. Very significant is the emphasis he puts on the halts in the march which, according to the commentary, perhaps showed most clearly what it was about (what it was for, rather than what it was against): the characteristic cutting from shot to shot of people resting at Turnham Green; the patient queuing for cups of tea; the young people dancing. 'Some people think that to dance is frivolous. But gaiety is part of this thing too. It's no use being against death if you don't know how to enjoy life when you've got it.'

Another important element is the questions that are asked but never answered – questions about the people who aren't marching. What are they for or against? The film is not particularly effective as propaganda, because it simply assumes that the sympathy of the audience is with the marchers, and not with these spectators. As the march approaches Aldermaston some onlookers are shown laughing: 'people who laughed as perhaps people laughed in Hiroshima before a small bomb exploded in the sky. Does an H-bomb have to explode here before we wake up?' There is in this the characteristic Anderson mixture of irony and compassion, but nothing to persuade the unbeliever. He is imposing not only his own pattern but his own viewpoint, working as an artist rather than a propagandist.

Drama

After the acknowledged success of *Thursday's Children*, which got some distribution in Britain as a result of winning an Oscar in 1955, Anderson had a number of offers that, for one reason or another, failed to materialise. A project to make a film about the horse on the farm fell through when he investigated the subject and said it should be about the tractor on the farm. He spent a few weeks in a centre in Croydon collecting material for a film about industrial rehabilitation for World Wide; this was co-sponsored by a Government department and Lever Brothers, and it collapsed when the two sponsors fell out. There was an idea for a film about the Rhondda Valley for the Central Office of Information: 'I wrote a script and they said they wanted something more like a newsreel.'

'Really, any subject I undertook I always wanted to turn into what I thought would be, in some way, a work of art,' he says. 'And in general this was what people did not want. It was typical that *Every Day Except Christmas*, for instance, when it started off was supposed to be a twenty-minute film and in fact was a forty-minute film. And it was only because of Leon Clore's imagination and generosity that the film was forty minutes, because, of course, Ford Motor Company didn't pay any more for it.'

Free Cinema was in Anderson's view 'always rather strongly resented by film-makers in this country and particularly by the old guard of documentary, none of whom ever did anything to help us. There were one or two friends like Basil Wright – but Basil wasn't really then producing films – and I would say that the documentary establishment were definitely hostile. They were hostile to our principles because we weren't a follow-on of the Grierson school. We were less sociological and propagandist than Grierson, and there wasn't much love lost between us.

'I would say that Free Cinema, almost from the start, was always and definitely is now better known outside Britain than in it. If I go to Cannes, for instance, I am asked questions about Free Cinema; if I go to Warsaw, I am asked questions about Free Cinema. In Britain they don't know what it is. There's a story, which I'm sure is true, about a representative of either the British Film Producers' Association or the British Council, who was asked by a journalist in an Eastern European country about Free Cinema. He looked up patiently and said "I don't think you understand that in Britain people have to pay to go to the cinema."

'When *Every Day Except Christmas* was submitted to the British selection board for the Venice Festival it was rejected by them. It had to be shown as a film for television, which it wasn't, in order to get into Venice. When it won the Grand Prix, the representative of the British film-makers' association was of course very annoyed. And there had been representations, I think from the Ambassador, at Venice to stop the film being shown, because they said it gave a very poor view of British life. This psychology is very close under the surface of today's enlightened attitudes. You've only got to look at the advertising for Britain to see that. I mean, how is Britain advertised abroad? It's advertised with pictures of beefeaters and the Queen at the Trooping of the Colour and timbered cottages, and this is still the image of Britain that's put out by British official sources. And to them to show a lot of scruffy Cockneys in Covent Garden market is in fact a bad advertisement for Britain. Exactly the same thing happened at Cannes with *If* . . . When the British Governmental representative had seen the picture he came to the stand of the British Film Producers' Association chattering with rage, and said it was disgusting that such a film should be shown.'

Shortly after *Every Day Except Christmas*, Anderson was approached by Ealing Studios to work on a feature project. He proposed filming a novel called 'Casualty', about young doctors in a casualty ward. (This was before the success on television of 'Emergency Ward 10'.) 'I was given a rather small sum to do a treatment for it, and I went to Guy's Hospital over a period of about a month or six weeks, and spent a lot of time with a white coat on in the casualty ward. I got quite a lot of background material, and I was interested in this subject and put forward an outline to them.

'They then said "We want some more romantic interest in the film." And I said "Well, I don't think that's my function. I couldn't write that sort of thing, but get a writer on to it, and I'll work with a writer." They refused to do this, and said I had to do it myself. I realised that this showed that their interest in me making such a film was really not serious, because if they'd been serious about it, of course they would have engaged a writer. So I said "Well, I'm not going to make any changes in it then." '

Rather than participate in this sort of 'very, very tepid, mild flirtation' with an industry which would at that time, he felt, accept him only on its terms, Anderson took up an invitation to direct 'The Long and the Short and the Tall' at the Royal Court Theatre. (At Tony Richardson's invitation he had previously done one Sunday night production, Kathleen Sully's 'The Waiting of Lester Abbs' for the English Stage Company at the Royal Court.) After the success of 'The Long and the Short and the Tall', he was invited to stay on at the Royal Court, where in the next few years he directed Alun Owen's 'Progress to the Park', John Arden's 'Serjeant Musgrave's Dance', Harry Cookson's and Christopher Logue's 'The Lily White Boys', Logue's 'Trials by Logue' and Max Frisch's 'The Fire Raisers'.

But, he remarks, 'when the idea for a film of "The Long and the Short and the Tall" came up, oddly enough to be made by Ealing, I wasn't of course rated as competent to direct it, since I'd only made documentaries and I'd only directed it on the stage. Nor for that matter was Peter O'Toole judged sufficiently striking or box office or whatever you like, to play the part which he created on the stage.'

This was just before *Saturday Night and Sunday Morning*, and Albert Finney was working with Anderson in the theatre in 'The Lily White Boys'. Finney, who was originally cast in the Peter O'Toole part in 'The Long and the Short and the Tall', would have worked with Anderson earlier had he not been ill, and it was probably Anderson who introduced him to Karel Reisz. By the time that *Saturday Night and Sunday Morning* opened (in late 1960), Anderson had directed Finney on the stage again in the title role in 'Billy Liar' at the Cambridge Theatre.

It was really the success of *Saturday Night and Sunday Morning* (made by Karel Reisz through the agency of Tony Richardson and Woodfall Films) that changed the climate of the British film industry sufficiently to accommodate a film-maker like Anderson.

'The position in those days,' he recalls, 'was that there had been one film, *Room at the Top*, which was hailed by the industry as a revolutionary breakthrough in British cinema. *Room at the Top* is, I think, a very good piece of film-making, but for that to be regarded as an adventurous breakthrough shows to what extent the British cinema was then antediluvian, because there was nothing in the social content of *Room at the Top* that wasn't in Warner Brothers pictures of the 1930's or a picture with somebody like John Garfield as a working-class hero. It was absolutely ludicrous that in Britain this should still be regarded as a breakthrough.

'You have to remember, however absurd it seems now and however much the middle-class critics continue to make jokes about working-class heroes, that in fact it really was as late as that before there had ever been a leading working-class character in a British film, apart perhaps from *Waterloo Road* during the war, which was sort of about Cockneys. The British cinema was really a bourgeois preserve, symbolised I suppose at its best by the middle-class tradition of Ealing.'

Saturday Night and Sunday Morning was a breakthrough not just in terms of social content, but in demonstrating that a picture with an unknown star and a director with no previous experience of feature film-making could make a commercial success. Resistance to new ideas, new faces, began to break down. And the sort of experience that Anderson had, in documentaries and in the theatre, at last began to qualify him to be thought of as a feature film-maker. It would probably have been only a matter of time until he made his first feature film.

Although Anderson believes that he was one of the first people to think about David Storey's novel 'This Sporting Life' as a likely film subject when it was first published in 1960, it was again largely due to chance, and what he has described as 'the grace and insistence of Karel Reisz', that he ended up making the picture. The film rights quickly became too expensive for Woodfall, which 'seemed at that time the only company likely to back me as a director'. But when the subject was bought by Julian Wintle and Leslie Parkyn of Independent Artists, they asked Karel Reisz to direct it, and Reisz, who after *Saturday Night and Sunday Morning* wanted some experience of producing, suggested that Anderson should direct with himself as producer.

'I remember our first meeting well, though not in detail,' Anderson wrote of David Storey in the programme for Storey's first play 'The Restoration of Arnold Middleton' (directed by Robert Kidd at the Royal Court in 1967). 'At that time I still believed, or wanted to believe that things (society) could become "better". David, whose father had not been some sort of General, and who had managed to fill out his Slade School Scholarship by battering and being battered, every Saturday during the Season as a forward in the Leeds Rugby League "A" team, was not under this misapprehension. Also he was not interested in surface, but in essence; not in what was representative, but in what was exceptional. This made him, and makes him, a very exceptional kind of English writer.

'A lot of glib generalisations have been made about the "Northern" writers who appeared in the late 'fifties and early 'sixties. In fact a certain kind of honesty, a certain kind of vitality is all they had in common. David Storey's unique quality – and it is one that I personally value above all others – seems to me a sort of elemental poetry, a passionate reaching-out, and ambition of concept that carries him beyond neatness, completeness, civilised equilibrium.

Still: Richard Harris as Frank Machin.

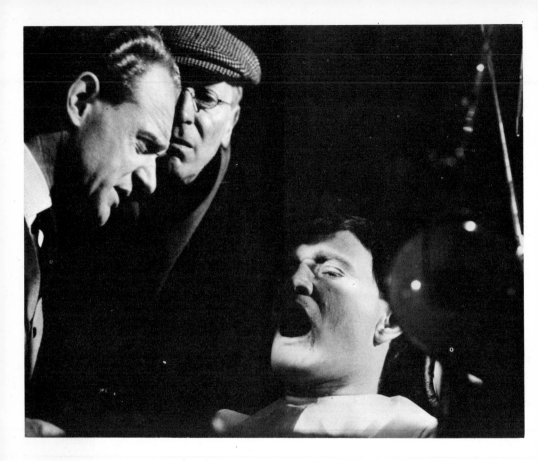

He seeks to penetrate the soul; yet he never forgets the relevance of the social world in which souls meet, conflict and struggle. He labours, often desperately, to balance the ambiguities of our nature, our situation: male and female, tenderness and violence, isolation and love.'

The note arguably describes the ambiguities of Anderson's own nature as much as Storey's – souls meeting in order to conflict, the

Still: the dentist (Frank Windsor), Johnson (William Hartnell) and Machin.

'battering and being battered' through which in seeming contradiction he expresses 'that within which passeth show'.

'I realised at once,' Anderson said of Storey's novel in an interview in *Films and Filming*, 'that this was something much more complex, and much more distinguished than the story of a footballer's success and disillusion which the advance note had suggested ... The central character, Frank Machin, was immensely striking, with an ambiguity of nature, half overbearing, half acutely sensitive, that fascinated me, without my being fully aware that I understood him. The same was true of his tortured, impossible relationship with the woman in the story; a bleak, Northern affair, of powerful, inarticulate emotions frustrated or deformed by puritanism and inhibition. The background rough and hard: no room here for charm or sentimental proletarianism. It was an intimidating subject for a film. I was not sure I would be up to it.'

In the same interview Anderson said that 'from the start, the film was essentially a collaborative affair. The book was such a personal piece of work that Karel and I both felt that no-one but its author could write the script ... David did all the writing, in between frequent and exhaustive consultations with Karel and myself.' While this was going on, they went to Yorkshire to look for locations in the places where Storey had grown up and set his novel, and it emerged that the young writer had been living about ten minutes' walk away from the Sutcliffe factory at the time that Anderson was making his first film there.

But the script was proving to be difficult. According to Anderson, it was not until Richard Harris entered into the collaboration that 'a conception emerged which began to satisfy us.' Anderson had decided that Harris was the right actor to play the lead in *This Sporting Life* after seeing him in the play of 'The Ginger Man' 'in which he gave a superb performance, a much more striking thing than he had ever had a chance to do on the screen'. Harris' contribution to the script seems to have been the suggestion that it should follow the book more closely than they had been doing.

The story is about rugby player Frank Machin (Arthur Machin in the book), and his affair with his widowed landlady, Mrs Hammond. Machin is a man who gets what he wants – usually by exploiting others – and his conflict is not with society but with himself, his own inarticulate and egocentric nature and, perhaps, his inability to shoulder any real responsibility. This personal conflict extends into his relationship with Mrs Hammond, an intense and puritanical woman, who lets him make love to her out of a kind of suppressed sensuality, but who refuses to enjoy it. She wants Machin either to go away or to marry her, because she is a conventional working-class woman and because marriage would imply a willingness to assume responsibility that Machin never shows. The situation assumes tragic proportions when Mrs Hammond, almost as an act of defiance, becomes ill and dies, and Machin too late discovers the tenderness that he was never able to extend to her before.

The construction of David Storey's script is very similar to that of his novel, which tells its story in the first person by means of a series of scenes or images that take us backwards and forwards in time. But the film is more consciously dramatic, less diffuse. It concentrates on the central conflict, omitting a number of subsidiary themes and relationships that are in the book, as well as something of the social and industrial background. Everything in the film is there specifically to illuminate the nature of the man Machin and his relationship with Mrs Hammond.

For the first two thirds of the film, past and present interweave. Then, picking up all the threads, the story moves towards its tragic climax. So at the beginning there are two time sequences. In the present, Machin is struck on the face during a rugby match, in a foul of the sort he had used in his first trial. He has six front teeth extracted under gas, goes to a Christmas Eve party at the house of Weaver (one of the two local industrialists who control the team) and then back home to Mrs Hammond.

The past emerges in flashback, not just while Machin is under gas but throughout the film up to the point where he comes home on Christmas Eve. It shows conversations with Mrs Hammond that go back to his early days in her house. It shows him getting his trial for the team and his £1,000 contract; driving home in a new white car; taking Mrs Hammond and her two children for an outing in the country; making love to her but failing to get an emotional response; visiting Mrs Weaver who unsuccessfully tries to seduce him.

At the point where past and present meet, the Weavers have fallen out with Machin. Weaver tells him that the only person now keeping him in the team is Slomer (the other industrialist who makes the team his hobby, and who initially disliked Machin's foul methods of play). The mood of the film shifts.

Stills: Christmas Eve. Below – Machin at the Weavers' party. Right – with Mrs. Hammond (Rachel Roberts).

Machin lurches along a railway line, watching a lighted train go by; the camera stays focused on a lamp standard against the night sky; a shot of Mrs Hammond's living room, festooned with Christmas decorations, is held until he enters it. Mrs Hammond has temporarily softened towards Machin, remembering her youth. She goes to bed with him.

After this the conflict with Mrs Hammond (already firmly established in the flashbacks) becomes increasingly overt. Machin takes her to a restaurant and she walks out because his behaviour is so egocentric. They go to his

friend Maurice's wedding and, behind the church, he strikes her face because she is ashamed of her position as his mistress, dolled up in the fur coat he has given her. At home they have a couple of increasingly violent rows, and he finally goes to a doss-house. He returns to find that she has been taken to hospital with a brain haemorrhage. He watches her die. The mood changes again as grief-stricken, he visits for the last time the familiar empty house: the bare bedstead, the oppressive wallpaper, the grimy skylight window. Then he is back on the football field playing a grey, hard game in

which he falls, is urged to get a move on, runs to join the others in the far distance.

As a feature film that necessitated collaborative work at every stage, *This Sporting Life* was obviously a totally different kind of undertaking from the documentaries for which Anderson wrote his own scripts, and which so clearly bear his individual stamp. It is the least personal of his serious films – a director's rather than an *auteur's* picture – and it links with his theatre work as much as with his earlier film-making.

In terms of toughness and maturity it takes a

Stills: Machin and Mrs. Hammond. Above – with her children and Johnson.

huge stride forward from *Every Day Except Christmas*, which it is astonishing to think was the last film that Anderson had directed before it. Nowhere in the earlier pictures was there this intensity, which arises in the first place from his collaboration with the actors and is then reinforced by the whole way the film is made, the camera set-ups and the editing. *This Sporting Life* is the most passionate film that has ever emerged from a British studio, and all

Anderson's previous experience in the theatre and cinema must have come into play to make it such a very remarkable feature film debut.

The impact begins with the performances. Interestingly Anderson approached the scenes between Richard Harris and Rachel Roberts (who plays Mrs Hammond) with what he has described as 'theatrical rather than traditional film method – rehearsing them for ten days before we started, continuing during evenings and weekends during shooting, taking them as far as possible in continuity on the floor.' This was fiction, but he brought to it, as he brings

to all his theatre work, the humanizing quality that made him such a fine documentary-maker.

Machin's way of tearing a paragraph about himself out of the local paper captures a good deal more of his personality than can easily be summed up in words: the largeness, impatience with neatness, unabashed self-esteem. Mrs Hammond is always busy with something (part of the self-denial that shapes her life) and the camera takes in the smallness of her actions, the actual nature of drudgery. As Machin's staunch friend Maurice, Colin Blakeley projects a character so firmly rooted in a real environment that the performance almost describes the environment.

Everywhere in the film, a particularly vivid kind of authenticity can be taken for granted, and yet it was, and still is, a very rare quality. Among British feature directors only Karel Reisz had approached anything as good as the pub scene in which Machin meets Maurice and two girls and entertains the locals with a flat rendering of 'Here in my heart'. Or the scene in which Machin gives Mrs Hammond the fur coat, and the neighbour who baby-sits tacitly registers her disapproval by turning her back

on them and rearranging things on the table. In his documentaries Anderson's way of showing people was always to pick out what was particular to individuals. In his first feature he puts the same kind of observation to dramatic use, pinpointing those qualities and aspects of behaviour that affect relationships and trigger off conflicts. His starting point is still naturalism.

This Sporting Life takes place in a tangible world of the senses. It shows feelings and is appropriately shot predominantly in close-up or medium shot. Anderson starts with the camera in the centre of a rugby game establishing at once the closeness, the immediacy that here characterises his whole dramatic approach, his determination to confront emotion directly, to involve and disturb us. And so the softness that finally surrounds Mrs Hammond's death in the novel has been omitted from the film, where the death scene is shot at clinically close quarters, a huge spider dropping behind the bed as the trickle of black blood oozes from Mrs Hammond's mouth, and Machin a moment later violently squashing the insect against the white wall with his bare fist (in Anderson's words 'the motif of force' that runs through the film). The film ends with a long-shot: Machin receding from the camera to join the rest of the rugby team at the other end of the field, and a kind of anonymity closing in on the character whose personal crisis has been played out with such painful intimacy.

Frank Machin is presented subjectively in the sense that we are shown his whole area of experience – where he is (even when he is unconscious in the dentist's chair), what he sees, thinks, remembers, feels. We are inside the character, and the construction of the film

Stills: the pub scene. Right – with Maurice (Colin Blakely).

is based on this idea – to reveal Machin without recourse to any of the usual artificial devices like interior monologues or voiced thoughts. Everything is shown. For example, in the novel Machin thinks about Mrs Hammond during his trial game: 'But her aggressive sort of indifference aroused in me a kind of anger, a savageness, that suited the game very well.' In the film, this is never put into words, but the link between Machin's relationship with Mrs Hammond and the kind of game he plays on the football field, is so clearly established from the outset that all the subsequent games add a

Stills: the death scene and after.

dimension to our understanding of him and of the relationship. After the happy outing in the country, the next cut is to a game in which he scores. A nightmare game, shown in slow motion in the mud, immediately precedes the sequence ending in Mrs Hammond's death.

The editing of the film is complex, linking the past with the present, and various aspects of the present with each other, in a boldly imaginative manner that made it so different from any British film of the period that some

audiences found it difficult to follow. The film would probably be appreciated rather more now than it was when it came out, because the influx of foreign films, particularly on television, has accustomed a wide audience to taking in its stride cutting techniques aimed not simply at telling a story but at evoking, by associations and juxtapositions, ideas and emotions integral to mood or theme. Anderson has always believed in over-estimating rather than under-estimating the acumen of his audience, so that there is in any case generally more in his films than anybody is likely to grasp at a single viewing.

The editing of *This Sporting Life* has an emotional as well as an intellectual logic. It shows the connections underneath the surface and therefore what the film is about. It also adds additional dimensions, which are taken up by Roberto Gerhard's score and by the use of overlapping sound, dialogue that precedes an image or carries over into the next scene. In this way it is always contributing to the tension and building up the picture's immense power.

When Machin is struck on the face during the football match at the beginning, a cut to him drilling for coal states the alternative to this tough game (spending the rest of his life as a miner) and also illustrates his momentary black-out as he hits the ground. When he is carried off the field and has his mouth sponged in the shower room, the film cuts to glimpses of Mrs Hammond and the children, the dead husband's boots which she keeps brightly polished on the hearth (all the scenes in her house are very close to the feeling of early D. H. Lawrence). And the physical unease carries over from one sequence to the other. Sometimes the juxtaposed sequences show parallel instances of Machin's behaviour so that we grasp his nature emotionally and instinctively without having it spelt out. For instance, during the night drive away from the dentist's, there are daylight tracking shots along a street that could have been in *Wakefield Express*, as Machin proudly takes his newly-purchased white car home. In the night shots he is also bearing gifts, Christmas presents for the children. He is generous but incapable of giving the things that matter, and of having the kind of relationship that extends beyond self.

In his attempts to live life to the full, Machin always limits and diminishes his own experience, as surely as Mrs Hammond does by her withdrawal into death. In an early scene, rather than take the opportunity to talk to her about her husband, he goes away and shadow boxes in his room. Later he generally substitutes violence for words, throwing something or hitting out at her. This reduction of everything there might have been between them, comes out in the editing too: the savage cut from his seduction of her to a shot of him grasping the bedpost and groaning, alone in an upstairs bedroom during the Weavers' party; the linking of his attitude to her with Mrs Weaver's chilling attempt to seduce him.

The way our sympathy is directed towards the characters in *This Sporting Life* is hard to explain. We share Machin's tragedy with him despite our awareness that he brought it on himself. We may even find ourselves occasionally out of sympathy with Mrs Hammond's self-righteousness and fussiness with the children. We are really carried far beyond the point where it is possible to describe the characters as sympathetic or unsympathetic, right or wrong. So few films have ever shown a complex adult relationship in these scrupulously adult terms, that our reactions to *This Sporting Life* can easily take us by surprise. But the most staggering thing about the picture was, and still is, its passionate emotion, the intensity of its anguish. 'Here pain *is* called pain,' wrote Robert Vas in *Sight and Sound*, 'and the feeling is one of liberation . . .'

The Poet

While they were still making *This Sporting Life*, Anderson and Harris had the idea of filming *Wuthering Heights* with Harris as Heathcliff. A script was actually written, and a good deal of time was spent on this. Then Harris' career carried him off to Hollywood, where he began to get leading parts, and the *Wuthering Heights* project never materialised. In the meantime, Anderson directed Harris in their own co-adaptation of Gogol's 'Diary of a Madman' at the Royal Court; then, as a guest director in Laurence Olivier's first season at the National Theatre, he directed Tom Courtenay in Max Frisch's 'Andorra'.

When *Wuthering Heights* finally fell through, Anderson started a season during 1964 and 1965 as joint artistic director with Anthony Page at the Royal Court Theatre, where he directed Shakespeare's 'Julius Caesar'. In 1966, the year that he made his mid-length film *The White Bus*, he was also invited by John Clements to direct 'The Cherry Orchard', with Celia Johnson and Tom Courtenay, at the Chichester Festival Theatre.

Part of a Woodfall trilogy subsequently called *Red, White and Zero, The White Bus* began as a project put up by Oscar Lewenstein, to which each of the Free Cinema directors – Anderson, Reisz and Richardson – was to make a contribution. Finding that his subject, *A Suitable Case for Treatment*, would run to feature length, Reisz withdrew it from the trilogy. He was replaced by Peter Brook as the third director. At this stage Richardson planned to film a short story 'Pavan for a Dead Prince' by Shelagh Delaney. Lewenstein proposed that the trilogy should consist of three Delaney subjects and offered Anderson *The White Bus*.

Anderson liked the subject and set to work on it with Shelagh Delaney, who wrote the script. Meanwhile, the others settled on non-Delaney subjects. Richardson eventually made *Red and Blue*, a film based on three songs with Vanessa Redgrave as its star, and Brook directed Zero Mostel in *The Ride of the Valkyries*. The resulting trilogy lacked a unifying theme, and its distributors, United Artists, put it on the shelf, suggesting that they would show the films separately when suitable opportunities arose.

Two years passed after the completion of *The White Bus*, and it still hadn't been shown. Anderson had started shooting *If ...* and, when asked the usual question (why he had made so few films), took to pointing out the fate of those that he had made already. Up to the time of writing, *The White Bus* has been shown publicly in Britain only for a brief run with Vera Chytilova's *Daisies* in South Kensington. 'It's obvious,' says Anderson, 'that a forty-five minute film of this kind is not something

55

that a major distributing company is the least interested in, or knows how to handle. There is a public for *The White Bus*, but not a public that, say, United Artists are in any way in touch with or know how to cope with. This is part of the whole problem of the major distributors, which grew up and were formed in relation to the Anglo-American (particularly the American) cinema of the 'twenties, 'thirties and 'forties, and still have that psychology. They are only very, very gradually gearing themselves to the public of the 'sixties and 'seventies. If such a film were in fact supported by the critics – in so far as the critics exist as a body – in an intelligent and constructive way, of course the result could be nothing but good. But the critics generally are just as much a part of the system as are the major distributors, so that as a film-maker one has no effective assistance from them. But it's probably a mistake to expect it. I mean, what are critics? Critics are simply the equivalents in journalism of the film distributors in the industry.'

The White Bus is the only film of Anderson's that has had a predominantly hostile reception from the critics, many of whom confined their displeasure to a few lines at the bottom of the column, which seems an odd way to treat the next film that he made after establishing himself as a director of major stature with *This Sporting Life*. Considering, too, the picture's ambitious and experimental nature as well as its relevance to contemporary life, the reviews arguably provide a good deal of evidence in support of Anderson's inveterate campaign against coterie attitudes and the Bloomsbury 'tradition of detachment from the problems of society'. He has always accused the 'bourgeois critics' of disliking reality and denying emotion.

Still: The White Bus. *The Girl (Patricia Healey) in her home town.*

And this kind of unresponsive attitude is one of the things that *The White Bus* is about.

Although the subject came to him almost by accident, Anderson has always seemed particularly keen on it. He has drawn attention to the theme recurring throughout his work – 'the tension between being alone and an almost nostalgic feeling of belonging to a group or community' – and also to the picture's ambiguity.

'I think I am very romantic, very idealistic by temperament, and perhaps I try to balance this with a certain irony and scepticism. I believe in ambiguity. *The White Bus*, for example, is the kind of film I wanted to make and am quite proud of having made. Some people find it a very sad film and some people find it a very satirical film. I hope it is both. I wouldn't dictate to anybody how they should receive it. Any work I have done, even if it has been very realistic, has always probably aimed for a poetic quality, and by poetic I mean suggestiveness. I mean the kind of work that in telling a story has bigger implications.'

As Anderson has also pointed out, the whole style of *The White Bus* clearly points towards *If* . . . Also it had the same cameraman, the young Czech Miroslav Ondricek, who had worked with Nemec, Forman and Passer, and in whom Anderson seems to have found the sensitivity that he requires in his collaborators.

The film shows a girl returning to her home town and joining an official conducted bus tour there. The girl in the story is Shelagh Delaney herself; in the film she is a typist in a London office, played by Patricia Healey who has an obvious physical resemblance to Shelagh Delaney.

The film starts on the Thames, a shot of a boy with a white dove on a barge, the office buildings, the girl typing late at her desk. A sudden, strange shot of her hanging from the ceiling, ignored by the cleaners working in the room, introduces a new element into Anderson's work.

This possible indication that the girl has no meaningful connections with her surroundings is fantasy, another way of looking at the world. The image encourages us to take things, not just literally, but with whatever added connotations the imagination can supply. During the film there are other images that are equally 'fantasy': the girl seen momentarily among the other girls in her old school singing 'Let us now praise famous men'; the people in a park who take up the attitudes of paintings by Manet, Goya, Fragonard; the bus passengers turned into tailor's dummies as they watch a civil defence demonstration.

The film is shot in black and white that splashes arbitrarily into splendidly rich colour from time to time. Anderson had never used colour before, and here too is something that encourages us to look at things in a fresh way. Life is always lived in colour, but most of us notice it only occasionally. The moments when we notice it are as inexplicable as the timing of the colour shots in this film, which express emotional textures, moods, the element of surprise that is a feature of being alive. Anderson's films increasingly show living at its most intense: the splendour, ruthlessness and pain of it. In the complex, elusive mixture of fantasy and reality that we find in *The White Bus*, he is feeling his way towards the violent position of *If* . . ., in which the two are interchangeable.

Apart from the fantasy shots in *The White Bus*, many of the images that represent apparent reality have an unreal quality. Here sound is used (or not used) in an organic way: the disturbing silence behind the procession of variously dedicated people wheeling a patient in an iron lung along the station platform when the girl arrives in her home town; the isolated footsteps of the running woman

Stills: the bus tour. Top – The Girl with the Macebearer (John Sharp). Above – passengers with the Mayor (Arthur Lowe) and the Conductress (Julie Perry).

whom she sees being openly abducted in the street. We are not just being shown that the ordinary is extraordinary; we are noticing the incongruity of making automatic assumptions, perhaps even questioning the validity of taking anything for granted.

The White Bus is about so many things, and contains within itself so many possible inter-

pretations, that writing about it is like putting up a succession of personal signposts. It is full of themes each of which have the kind of universality that is limited by being described in terms of one person's experience. Hence, although the technique could in general be described as a comic one, for me the film is not primarily a comedy.

My response begins with the theme of the girl's isolation. The transitions into fantasy and into colour, from sadness to humour, from nostalgia to satire, show her mixed feelings about a world in which she feels cut off from other people, and therefore finds their behaviour often fantastic, idiotic or merely futile. The oblique and shifting tensions of the film are a kind of reaching out for contact and a closing in upon herself again. Her alienation is something actual, not a neurosis; like many working-class people whom an increasingly bureaucratic society has separated from their roots, she has no sense of belonging anywhere.

At the end of the film she wanders alone through lamplit streets, seeing behind lighted windows people whose lives have a meaning that hers has lost: a child pianist immersed in her music, an old woman devotedly shaving an old man. She ends up in a fish and chip shop, where an assistant, erecting a forest of upturned chairs on the tables all around her, recites a repetitive speech about the way that routine work goes on identically from one day to the next.

Then there is the satire on provincialism. But unless you realise that the provinces are everywhere, and find satire and compassion not incompatible, you are liable to lose much of the point of this. The obvious satire is at its sharpest in the characterisation of the tour's official spokesmen: the bus conductress, reciting her facts and statistics quite without expression; the Mayor (who complacently tours his own town with the mace-bearer)

airing his special gift for rhetoric. Arthur Lowe, as the Mayor, gives a precise, hilarious parody of smug parochialism, full of unthinking echoes from the higher corridors of power. But the character is too unaware of his own limitations (his bigotry, narrow-mindedness, acute philistinism), too human to be totally unsympathetic. We laugh and feel superior in much the same way as Alice felt superior to some of the equally self-satisfied humbugs she met in Wonderland.

The way in which the satire extends to the other passengers on the white bus raises a great

Still: the bus passengers watching the Civil Defence demonstration.

many questions. These are provincial people from various parts of the world – they include a Japanese woman and a Nigerian man in national costumes, and a bowler-hatted British businessman – and they are shown with that mixture of emotions peculiar to Anderson. There is mockery and tenderness, affection and irony, and audiences can really react according to their disposition. Yet, like the trippers in *O Dreamland*, these tourists are totally lacking in initiative and enterprise. They have chosen to be herded around like sheep, and appear to regard most of what they see with unimaginative impassivity – an impassivity that we are never allowed to share. We are constantly assailed by striking visual contrasts, from towering blocks of flats to affluent suburban houses, from industrial landscapes and factory buildings to the parkland surrounding a once stately home. We are struck by the richness and variety of local industry and recreations that include the making of pottery, tapestry and cakes as well as all the opportunities afforded by the public library, museum, art gallery and the ideas invoked by a Brechtian song.

If all this means next to nothing to the tourists why have they come on the white bus? Why do people go on conducted tours? Why do they visit museums, art galleries, grope about in search of 'culture'? Is this not an extension of the attitude that makes them want to be together, to do things in groups? Is it not all part of a need to communicate? The passengers on the white bus are shown very differently from the trippers in *O Dreamland*. Anderson is standing farther back now, aware of the complexity of their predicament, seeing all round it.

From this another theme emerges: the effect of a conformist society on the individual's ability to react emotionally, aesthetically, morally to anything. Watching a very realistic civil defence demonstration, all the tourists except the girl turn into dummies: their last stand against making any kind of direct response. This is what comes of taking things too literally. The poor tourists no longer exist. Conformity has blanked them out.

During the civil defence demonstration there are shots very reminiscent of Jennings' *Fires Were Started*, but these are not mere references or *hommages*; they momentarily evoke the actual spirit of the war, connecting and contrasting it with that of Britain in the 'sixties. What is important is that we are experiencing both situations together; we are responding to something which we know to be unreal in the context of today, and which is nonetheless more real than the defence demonstration itself and than society's related acceptance of the bomb.

The White Bus contains such a wealth of implication that it seems a slightly different film each time you see it. It is only to be hoped that, before long, a few more people will get the chance of seeing it at least once.

Anderson's next film was made at the invitation of the Warsaw Documentary Studios as a souvenir of a visit to Poland. He was there directing Tadeusz Lomnicki in John Osborne's 'Inadmissible Evidence' at the Contemporary Theatre in Warsaw in 1966. Anderson first met Lomnicki, whom he had seen in Wajda's *A Generation* at the 1957 Cannes Film Festival, when he visited Poland for the BBC around that time; and Lomnicki had for some years had the idea that Anderson might direct him as Hamlet in Warsaw. It was with that intention that Anderson actually went to Warsaw, but a contemporary play was finally preferred.

The film that the Documentary Studios invited him to make was another project like *Every Day Except Christmas*, where there was a possibility of doing anything. Anderson found his subject when his assistant at the theatre, who also worked for Professor Ludwik Sempolinski at the Warsaw Dramatic Academy, persuaded him to spend an afternoon watching the Professor instructing a class of third year students. That afternoon Anderson saw three of the six songs from which, with the same students, he made his twenty-minute film *Raz Dwa Trzy* (*The Singing Lesson*) in 1967. Anderson was offered a number of older cameramen who spoke English, but asked for a young cameraman and was introduced to Zygmunt Samosiuk, whom he liked and decided to work with. Samosiuk had no English. Before embarking on the film, he spent some time looking at Warsaw with Samosiuk, getting to know it, and finding the images that he cut into the song sequences. The film took about two and a half to three weeks to shoot.

'The frustrations of working in Poland are different from the frustrations in Britain,' Anderson commented afterwards. 'There the techniques are apt to be extremely primitive and the resources are primitive. But they aren't over-organised as I think we are in this country, so that there is a kind of personal nature to the work throughout.' He added, however, that if he were making something more ambitious in Poland he would probably be more frustrated than he is in Britain: 'The political pressures are so strong that in fact it's practically impossible to make a really serious feature film in Poland at the moment.'

According to its foreword, *The Singing Lesson* is 'a sketchbook or a poem. The words of the songs are not important, only their themes and the images and memories they evoke.'

Anderson's two short films of the 'sixties are realistic in a way that was only hinted at in the documentaries of the 'fifties. The idealistic viewpoint is now consistently shown in conjunction with its opposite. Cynicism (my word; Anderson disclaims any such attitude. 'I'm not cynical. I'm just realistic,' he says), disillusionment, an acceptance of what he once called 'the murky and undecided realities of today' are an intrinsic part of the vision. The kind of confrontation that occurred in the café scene in *Every Day Except Christmas* has become a dominant theme.

In his crusading days, in *O Dreamland* and *Every Day Except Christmas*, he was generally isolating particular aspects of the world in order to show variations on a single theme. These more mature films differ too in each containing innumerable themes, in being about a great many things at the same time.

The Singing Lesson is about innocence and experience, about youth seen through its own eyes and through the eyes of maturity, about youth looking out at the sad world it has inherited and the everyday world with which it has still to come to terms, about the relationship between art and reality, about the way reality shifts according to the experience of every individual and each generation.

All this grows out of something that appears to be simplicity itself: an affectionate impression of some Polish students rehearsing song and dance routines with their elderly professor in a classroom, intercut with shots of the ordinary life going on in the streets and shops outside. The songs, each with a different mood – sad, vibrant, pensive, urbane, sentimental, exuberant – flow into each other, and out into the world beyond so naturally that it is easily possible not to notice the rich complexity of the film's structure. Emotionally it works in very much the same way as Jennings' *Listen to Britain*, but Anderson is finding his symbols in a world where issues are less clear-cut and brave causes exist only in the history evoked by song. 'I cried Help! Help! – no one came,' reads one of the very few subtitles. *The Singing Lesson* is about individual survival in a world that impersonal forces increasingly command.

All the elements of the situation in the film are welded together before and during the first song 'The Coat' which, according to the subtitle, tells 'of Poland's inheritance, of the winds of history that buffet its people . . .' Behind the credits the clapper-board is raised in front of the stage. But as the song begins we are not in the classroom, but watching a train pulling into a railway station, and during the

Frames: The Singing Lesson – '*The Coat*'.

song the film cuts back to the anonymous crowds at the station, and also to street scenes, buildings, memorials and (in a moment of silence) to images evoking wartime suffering: empty bowls, the photograph of a man with haunted eyes, a list of names and dates.

This is the other background against which the boy sings, and towards which everybody in the room is also looking. But they each have a different vantage point, and from the beginning the film shows this by the different positions taken up by the camera, and by the cutting, from the pianist to the singer to the class with the professor and back to the singer again. Then a student comes in late from a Warsaw that for him centres on this room, and everybody's attention is momentarily distracted from the singer and their own thoughts, as the camera observes this boy taking off his coat and sitting down beside the others. We are pulled back to the classroom by ordinary human details that contrast with the romantic fantasy of the students' performances.

The film brings together actualities separated by place and time but equally part of the fabric of experience. We are looking at players on a stage, and at people looking at players on a stage, and at the everyday world outside (the real world?) and at the way that history marks people and their environment. And all these things are interwoven to heighten our apprehension of each and to create a new experience.

The images that link the songs are always outside the classroom: old and new buildings,

Frames: Below – 'Big Beat'. Right – 'A Lullaby – for those who wait'.

lamp standards, modern blocks of flats, an art exhibition, the pavements and trees of Warsaw, a cat against a stucco wall, an ornate interior to introduce the final *fin de siècle* number. These shots are part of the whole pattern of ideas and images running through the film. They make it a unity rather than a succession of individual songs.

The second number 'Big Beat' is sung and danced by a boy in a checked shirt and a girl in mini-skirt and boots. The repetitions of the music connect outwards with shoals of patterned umbrellas and cars and people in the rainy streets; a cloakroom attendant hangs up coats and coats and still more coats.

In the third song 'A Lullaby – for those who wait' the animated faces in the classroom alternate with those of women in shops waiting, without interest, to serve and to be served. In a china shop a customer stares blankly into space. From close-ups of the expressive girl singer, the film cuts to shopgirls, dignified, patient, waiting like statues for nothing to happen. Sitting behind the counter in a souvenir shop a middle-aged woman looks directly at the camera, defying us to fathom an expression of alienation strangely reminiscent of the man who did the same thing in the café scene in *Every Day Except Christmas*. The sequence that follows, of people sleeping in waiting rooms, has a number of shots that are positioned in exactly the same way as the similar passage in the earlier film. This is Anderson's particular no-man's-land, the area where individual nostalgias isolate people in transit and people in crowds.

'Sunshine Street' is a gay, impeccably upper middle-class song about the idiotic bourgeoisie, waited on by shop assistants and commissionaires, trying on hats and coats in fashionable department stores, parading in front of mirrors, adjusting their hair and make-up, eating ices in a restaurant where the exquisitely folded table napkin merits a close-up for its own sake.

During 'Sweet Peas', a song from the gardener's boy to his love, the camera never

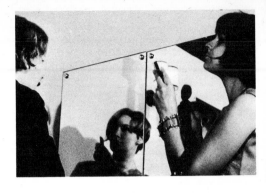

leaves the classroom. The film cuts backwards and forwards from shots of the singer to close-ups of girls' faces in the room. By now we are projecting our own impressions on the white backcloth behind the stage, reading our own fantasies into the romantic song.

Frames. Opposite page: top – 'Sunshine Street';
bottom left – 'Sweet Peas'; bottom right and this
page 'Oh, Miss Sabina!' .

The last number 'Oh, Miss Sabina!' begins
inside the classroom with a dialogue between
two students in turn-of-the-century costumes,
and the professor intervening to demonstrate
how the boy's part should be played. A short
speeded-up sequence strikes a comic note that
is out of character with the rest of the film
unless it is regarded as a way of stressing the
artificiality of the set-up and, by contrast, the
increasing naturalism that follows, when the
professor takes a partner, and everybody in the
room begins to dance. And the music washes
outwards over the rush-hour crowds in Warsaw:
men and women with tired, preoccupied faces
heading for home, one of them clutching a long,
thin bunch of flowers.

If...

Then I asked: 'does a firm perswasion that a thing is so, make it so?'

He replied: 'All poets believe that it does, and in ages of imagination this firm perswasion removed mountains; but many are not capable of a firm perswasion of any thing.'

Blake: *The Marriage of Heaven and Hell.*

By the time he made *The Singing Lesson*, Anderson was already working with David Sherwin on the script of *If* . . . The original film treatment, *Crusaders*, had been brought to his attention in September 1966 by Seth Holt, who then intended to produce. Anderson has said that he was first attracted to the subject by the title *Crusaders* 'with its overtones of idealism, struggle and the world well lost. "Charge once more then and be dumb . . .".' He was always attracted towards the kind of heroism that ends in defeat but is not defeatist: Ford's heroes in *They Were Expendable* remaining 'indomitable in disaster'; the spirit of the boy in Wajda's *A Generation* 'who jumps to his death rather than be caught or killed by the Germans, raising his hand before he goes, in a last, fine salute to life.'

The story of *Crusaders* had begun eight years before. David Sherwin and his friend John Howlett, who were at public school together, began to work on it when they went up to Oxford in 1958, and completed a first draft by the spring of 1960. Five years passed before they found an interested producer in Seth Holt. At this point Holt took Howlett to Rome to work on another project, and left Sherwin in Britain revising *Crusaders*.

When Anderson, at Holt's invitation, agreed to direct the film, Howlett was still in Rome, so that the final screenplay was written by Sherwin, who worked on it with Anderson during most of 1967. At this time it acquired a different ending, for Sherwin, who has likened his hero to Buchner's Woyzeck, first envisaged the violent climax in terms of suicide.

'I put a lot of myself into *If* . . .' Anderson said in an interview for *Le Monde* in 1969. 'It is largely autobiographical.' As he has also claimed that he enjoyed his own schooldays which 'passed off rather quietly and in a quite civilised way', the remark cannot be taken literally. It means something rather more fundamental about the way he has committed and revealed himself in his most personal film.

Seth Holt became too occupied in directing his own films to continue as producer, and Anderson took the subject to Memorial Enterprises, the Company formed by Albert Finney and headed by Michael Medwin, where it was received with open arms. Distributors, however, were less enthusiastic – particularly

Still: the school chapel in If . . .

British ones. 'Shapeless; no story line; will they care in Wigan? There are no parts to offer Julie Christie or Mike Caine. What about Sir Laurence as the Headmaster? Or Sir John, or Sir Michael, Sir Alec or Sir Ralph? Can you shoot it in six weeks?' (Anderson, who co-produced with Medwin, described their reactions in a characteristic tilt at the whole set-up that appeared in The Observer a few days before the opening).

The American company CBS, which had just set up a films division, were the first to show an interest in If . . . They accepted the subject and then backed out about six weeks before shooting was due to commence. Nobody knew why, but it was suggested that someone in California had finally got round to reading the script. Paramount came to the rescue. Within forty-eight hours they had agreed to take over the whole thing. This has been variously represented as an act of faith in Anderson, in the subject itself and (by realists) in Albert Finney.

If . . . is set in what Anderson has described as 'a fictitious, but extremely authentic public school', and shows how three rebels are finally driven into staging a violent revolt against

70

Photographs: the making of If . . . *Anderson with Miroslav Ondricek (left) and Michael Newport as Brunning (above).*

everything the place stands for. The archetypal school, shown in the film, is in fact an amalgam of three schools – one of them being Anderson's old school Cheltenham College, where, during term-time, the revolution was filmed.

This archetypal English public school is Anderson's own beginning. And the similarity in the film between what is internal and what is external, what is stated and what is suggested, starts here, in this community of boys in whom the men they will become are already identifiable. Schools like this one are still the training ground for a preponderance of top jobs in every sphere of authority in the country, the cradle of traditions peculiarly British. Anderson's profound patriotism (linking here with his affection for his old school) has always been evident in recurrent attacks on the stereotyped image of his country that others are content to present to the world. His picture of this school is at the same time savage about the system, and full of love for the culture that it stands for and that made him what he is. This ambiguity also extends outwards. He was attracted, he says, by 'the extent to which school is a microcosm – particularly in England where the educational system is such an exact image of the social system'. He wanted to show 'a little or a limited world which has implications about the big world and about life in general'.

Filming began in March 1968. The budget (£250,000 in all) was a modest one, and it was decided at the outset to economise on the number of locations that would have to be repainted, as well as on colour stock, by shooting certain scenes in black and white. Had it not been for the absolute compulsion to make a colour film (for eventual showing on American television), Anderson, who has very little confidence in his own colour sense, would have chosen monochrome. In the event, he relied very much on his production designer Jocelyn Herbert and on Miroslav Ondricek to ensure consistency of colour design over the various locations. Both were people with whom he had previously collaborated. Jocelyn Herbert had often worked with him at the Royal Court Theatre, and Ondricek was asked to come from Prague again as a result of the happy collaboration on The White Bus.

The shooting schedule (upwards of ten weeks) left no time for trial and error, or the kind of over-shooting that Anderson in any case considers an indulgence. The second draft shooting script, completed towards the end of 1967, had been worked out to be practically foolproof, and was followed very closely during shooting and editing. It contained, however, no descriptions of camera angles or movements; all this was worked out on the floor, often as a result of intuitive consultations (unintelligible to anybody else) between Anderson and Ondricek.

'The director seemed to be reluctant to discuss the shooting script with me at the beginning, or to talk about editing,' the film editor David Gladwell has since written in an article in 'Screen'. 'This I have since come to recognise as typical Anderson. One is expected to feel, to deduce, to infer, but never to need an explanation, even at the basic level when working together. At my first meeting with him, he made it clear that it would be he and not I who would be editing the picture . . .'

Stills: below – Cheltenham College, the setting of If . . . Right – Anderson, with Nicol Williamson, in Inadmissible Evidence.

In describing his first experience of cutting a scene for Anderson, who was on location at the time and wanted to make sure he hadn't undershot, Gladwell gives a very clear impression of Anderson's method:

'The script seemed a little vague at this point, and so I cut the shots together in an attempt to make something "begin to work". The result looked rather unsatisfactory. There was no time then to work longer on the sequence, and so I had to let it go as it was . . . I learned later of his explosion on viewing my attempt and of his outspoken opinion of editors; but to me he merely complained that I had made it look like a scene from an Ealing comedy – "far too many cuts," he said, "try putting it together to follow the script." The scene takes place during the Field Day of the College Cadet Force when the three rebels cause chaos and panic by firing into the tea-queue. In four short statements the script described what happens. It was this simplicity which I had mistaken for vagueness, and it was this simplicity which the director required in his film.'

Anderson's unusual clarity of mind is something that he can, if he wishes, project into his working relationships. This applies particularly to actors towards whom he always extends that consideration and innate respect for people that is the affirmatory side of his temperament and his work. (He is himself a member of Actors Equity, and plays small parts from time to time; his two latest appearances have been as a cynical Gestapo lawyer in David Mercer's television play 'The Parachute' and as a bad-tempered barrister in the film of Osborne's *Inadmissible Evidence*, both directed by Anthony Page.)

Deprecating the assumption that performances are created by the director, he emphasises the importance of casting actors for the precise qualities of personality required in the part. In this way he repeatedly uncovers acting potential that it is in the nature of any system that relies on the safe and the familiar to pass by. To quote from the Free Cinema credo again: 'An attitude means a style. A style means an attitude.' Anderson's attitude to actors (an attitude that gives to some of the performances in *If . . .* a psychological depth well beyond the possible experience of the young people playing the roles) is as much a part of his style as the creative process that continues later in the cutting rooms.

By the time he made his first feature film, Anderson's contempt for critics seemed to

stem largely from irritation at the improbability of any critic ever indicating that he had got as much out of Anderson's work as the director knew he had put into it. ('One can imagine criticism so perceptive and illuminating that it can also illuminate the artist, show him what he has been doing, and tell him truths about himself he did not see. But in practice one seems to know the faults and virtues of what one has done more clearly than the people who

Still: the beginning of term.

criticise it.') Consequently when interviewed about both his feature films, he would begin by claiming a certain difficulty, as an artist, in saying what the film was about. ('Because, in fact, that is talking or thinking like a critic. One doesn't start, at the beginning, to make a film about anything. One starts with an intuition or an impulse and a subject and an area of experience, and whatever one makes grows out of that.') Then somehow he would end up really talking like a critic, and describing what his work was about a good deal more articulately and persuasively than anybody else.

In interviews and conversations of this kind, Anderson is rarely just describing his intentions. He is more often interpreting the finished work in precisely the way that he argues a good critic should. The capacity to do this is unusual in a film-maker, and not something to be ignored.

'The older you grow, the more you are conscious of and believe in and have to accept the ambiguities of existence,' Anderson said shortly after making *If* . . . 'And you know that in every truth the opposite is also true. The very important thing is to perceive *that* truth, and yet hold the opposite of *that* truth, which is that there *is* a truth.'

The opposites have always been apparent in his work. Idealism is an extreme position, increasingly hard to maintain as time brings experience of what Bertrand Russell has described as 'the major evils to which life is subject; the treachery of friends, the death of those whom we love, the discovery of the cruelty that lurks in average human nature.' In Anderson's work the opposites of idealism (cynicism, compromise, defeatism, apathy) are increasingly perceived.

It is also out of a conflict of opposites that he creates. As he once put it 'The artist must always bite the hand that feeds him. He must always aim beyond the limits of tolerance. His duty is to be a monster.' The humanitarianism combines with the ruthlessness bound up with artistic survival. The truth to which the artist still holds is in the work of art. In *If* . . . the same truth emerges from the thing said and the way it is said. In form and content there are the same wildly funny and yet recognisably realistic contradictions of existence.

The film is constructed in a series of short scenes which come under eight chapter headings. In the way that the picture cuts from scene to scene, ideas are constantly set up in opposition to each other so that stylistically as well as logically we are moving steadily towards the violent explosion at the end. Of the chapters Anderson said to Claude Delmas of *Jeune Cinéma:* 'When I worked on the original script with David Sherwin, we divided it into chapters. I think that from the beginning I felt that *If* . . . would be an epic film in the Brechtian sense of the word, so there had to be in it a strong element of objectivity, as there must be in a film aimed at the understanding. *If* . . . is not meant to be a film that excites or agitates, but I hope that people understand it; this is why the division into chapters and, up to a certain point, the use of black and white and colour, are what Brecht calls processes of distanciation which detach the spectator from his emotion . . . For me, the essential problem today is that of the relation between the individual and the technological society, and this is why capitalist-communist problems are in fact out of date; in other words, the problem applies as much to one system as to the other, and that is why a film like *If* . . . will be understood by both; certainly in this sense I think that *If* . . . is a rather Brechtian film.'

The chapters begin with exterior shots of the green playing fields or imposingly serene school buildings, and of the chapel where aspiration and emotion are daily channelled into the communal singing of morning hymns. There is in these tableaux, and in the organ music and the hymns enlarging the emotional experience, not just a distancing effect but the stillness and the timeless quality of recollections that remain with people for life: the core of that nostalgia that Anderson himself, perhaps more than most people, feels for his schooldays, the nostalgia for a lost community life that is a recurrent theme throughout his work. But the inherent

76

contradictions are universal: the attachment to old roots and memories shackles people, so that progress always means a kind of destruction.

Boys arrive in College House for the Winter Term, read the notice board in the corridor and disperse to common rooms, studies and dormitories to unpack. In the hierarchy new boys are Scum or what at other schools might be called fags; authority is represented by four Whips or prefects led by Rowntree (Robert Swann), always impeccable in a floral waistcoat, who is Head of House. 'Run in the corridor!' he shouts, and orders a Scum to warm a lavatory seat for him. From the beginning there is a calculated lunacy about this real environment that could be regarded as pushing towards fantasy.

Mick the rebel (Malcolm McDowell), a senior boy, hiding the moustache grown in the holidays under a scarf wound round his jaw, appears in a get-up closely resembling that of Ivor Novello in Hitchcock's *The Lodger*. 'When do we live?' he says to his friend Johnny (David Wood) as the bell summons them to a ceremony of initiation in the dining hall; speeches from Kemp the Housemaster (Arthur Lowe) and Rowntree are followed by a medical inspection: 'Health certificate? Ringworm? Eye disease? V.D.? Confirmation class?' The Matron (played with unctuously maternal sensuality by Mona Washbourne) examines each boy's penis with a torch. It could happen of course, but the question about V.D. and the torch carry that hint of fantasy which is finally what makes the scene so funny. Sexual suppression is part of

Stills: the medical inspection. Left – at the head table (left to right) Barnes (Peter Sproule), Fortinbras (Michael Cadman), Denson (Hugh Thomas), Rowntree (Robert Swann), John Thomas (Ben Aris), Mr Kemp (Arthur Lowe), Mrs Kemp (Mary MacLeod) and the Matron (Mona Washbourne).

the atmosphere of the place. In a strange, inhibited scene (the first in monochrome) the housemaster's frustrated wife, who later takes the opportunity to stalk naked through the corridors when the boys go out on a field exercise, demurely directs the new under-master, John Thomas, to her bedroom. 'Whatever you're doing now. Don't,' Mick whispers to the spotty Stephens in the darkened dormitory.

Lessons begin. Mick, it emerges during the first history class, is clever. ('What is perplexing to so many of us is that normal, straightforward, friendly and decent young men suddenly kick over the traces in ways which we are forced to take seriously,' the Headmaster of Malvern was quoted as saying in connection with the new phenomenon known as Sixth Form Rebellion in the magazine *Where?* in 1964. And there is, incidentally, ample evidence in the recent report of the Public Schools Commission and in a Factual Survey sponsored by the

Headmasters Conference in 1966, to substantiate the authenticity of most of the background in *If . . .*)

The Chaplain, taking a geometry lesson, pauses to twist the nipple of the new boy, who is shortly subjected by his immediate seniors to a test of his proficiency in school slang. 'You do realise it's not just a matter of knowing the answers. It's how you say it. One word wrong and you'll fail the whole test.' This is the position that every system, by being a system and therefore resisting change, must ultimately reach. Juxtaposed with it is the Headmaster's image of the school: 'College is a symbol of many things. Scholarship, integrity in public office, high standards in the television and entertainment worlds, huge sacrifice in Britain's wars.' It is because what he says is true that he represents precisely the kind of allegedly progressive 'liberal' that Anderson has always

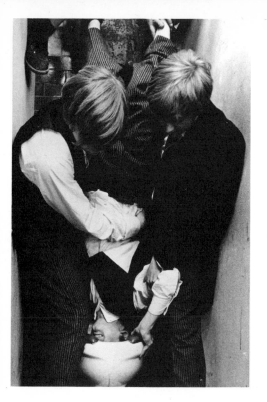

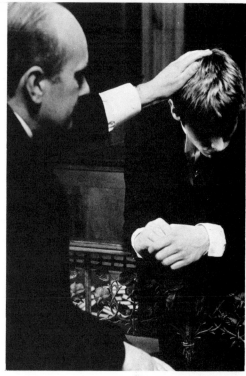

Stills : opposite – the geometry lesson with the Chaplain (Geoffrey Chater) and Jute (Sean Bury). Above – the lavatory scene. Right – the Chaplain with Stephans (Guy Ross).

opposed as the worst enemy of real progress. Anderson's contempt for what is merely fashionable comes under the same heading. Fashion is, after all, a way in which society superficially changes in order to remain radically the same. The Headmaster in *If . . .* is a man who moves with the times, a key figure in the streamlined technocratic society.

Mick lets off steam by pinning pictures from magazines (adolescent symbols of freedom and violence) to his study wall, and listening to the primitive music of a Congolese mass on his record-player. Biles, the boy nicknamed 'the freak', is pursued and hung upside down in the lavatory. But the juniors are learning the school song, 'Stand Up! Stand Up! for College', and Stephans, confessing his dirty thoughts to the Chaplain, is being urged to 'fight the good fight'. The system repeatedly links religion with militarism in a way that negates belief in an independent truth. The establishment has appropriated the best symbols, the best words for battle. By comparison with what college stands for Mick's collages seem tawdry, second-rate. 'That affirmation should have become the prerogative of politicians and blurb-writers is shameful,' wrote Anderson many years before. 'But this means that belief has to be rescued, not that it must be abandoned.'

Term sets in. Rowntree gives his very attractive Scum Bobby Philips as a temptation to his fellow Whip, Denson (Hugh Thomas), whose puritanical veneer fails to conceal a deep yearning. The three rebels, Mick, Johnny and Wallace (Richard Warwick), drink Vodka together. 'Violence and revolution are the only pure acts,' says Mick. Denson sentences the trio to cold showers because their hair is too long.

Symbolic acts of love and war take place in the gymnasium: a very romantic sequence intercuts shots of Wallace performing on the horizontal bar with shots of Bobby Philips putting on his sweater (the dawn of an attachment between the two); in a fencing match with Johnny and Wallace 'real blood' is drawn from Mick. Instead of attending a College rugger

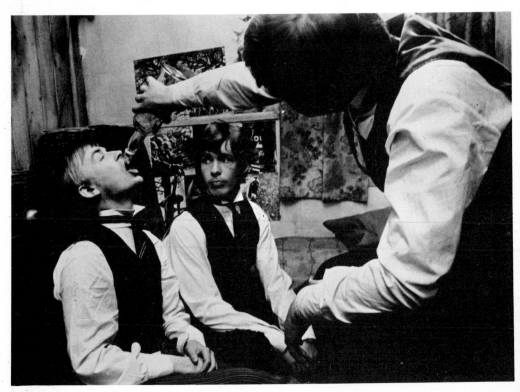

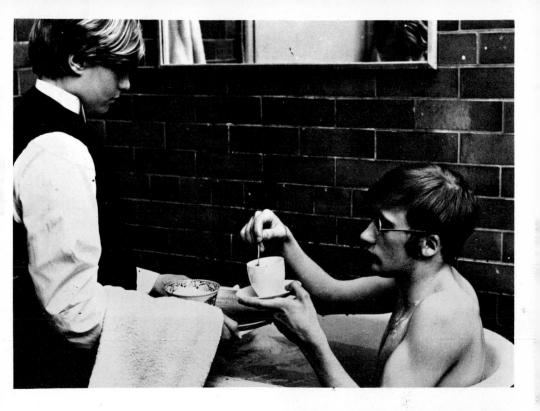

Stills: left – the rebels, Johnny (David Wood), Wallace (Richard Warwick) and Mick (Malcolm McDowell). Above – Bobby Philips (Rupert Webster) and Denson. Right – 'real blood'.

match, Mick and Johnny break bounds, steal a motor bike and ride off to the Packhorse Café. Suddenly Mick and the girl who serves them coffee (Christine Noonan) are growling at each other like tigers, and rolling naked on the floor.

For some people this is the point in the film where realism turns to fantasy, a feeling that is perhaps enhanced by the fact that the scene is

shot in black and white (although the use of colour and black and white is obviously not directly related to the idea of fantasy and reality in the rest of the film). But the impression of a relationship here is actually no less realistic than that of everyday behaviour in some of the earlier bizarre and cruel school scenes, which the same people laughingly accept as real. All rituals are a kind of fantasy that people have imposed upon themselves as a defence against

Stills: Mick and Johnny break bounds. Right – in the café with the Girl (Christine Noonan).

the real and primitive impulses that lead to destruction. This destruction is the climax of *If . . .* , and the film could be interpreted as being about the way in which people blind themselves to reality, cut themselves off from emotion, refuse to see both life and death as they really are. The threshold between fantasy and reality in the film is then something that must vary according to how much reality the individual spectator can bear. And the film's supreme achievement is in enabling audiences to interpret it according to their own idea of what is real. Undoubtedly, some people find a

lot of fantasy in *If* . . . For others, like Anderson himself, 'it's all real.'

After the café incident, the system takes its revenge, which characteristically is not called revenge. The Housemaster, weak politician that he is, washes his hands of the whole business; and the Whips beat the rebels not for any specific misdemeanour, but for being a general nuisance. ('The boys are beaten actually for what they are,' says Anderson, citing this as an instance of the way in which the film is epic in the Brechtian sense. 'The concern is much more to show what people are, what things actually are, than to tie everything together in a specific cause and effect.') Asked if he has anything to say, Mick delivers a speech worthy of his spiritual forbear Jimmy Porter: 'The thing I hate about you, Rowntree, is the way you give Coca-Cola to your Scum and your best teddy bear to Oxfam . . . and expect us to

Stills: left and above – the beating. Right – the field exercise: 'the yell of hate' and the shooting of the Chaplain.

lick your frigid fingers for the rest of your frigid life.' The beating that he gets is commensurate with the magnitude of this offence.

The rebels' mingle blood in a ceremony of solidarity, but the first signs of resistance are the bullets that puncture the tea-urn during the Cadet Force field exercise. The usually quiet and intellectually inquiring Peanuts had been demonstrating 'the yell of hate' – 'the yell that counts' in the same way as knowing not just the answers but how to say it, counts. John Thomas had been idiotically pretending to shoot a lot of people dead. Then suddenly the game intensifies when Mick shoots and bayonets the frightened Chaplain who had ridden out so vaingloriously at the head of his forces such a short time before. 'I

take this seriously,' says the Headmaster, ludicrously resurrecting the representative of the church from a drawer in his study. All through the film there is an uncertainty about what is fantasy except here. For me, this *must* be fantasy. 'Harold Pinter got very upset about that moment,' says Anderson. 'He thought it got very out of style. He may well be right.' It is interesting of course that the Chaplain isn't dead or gored, in the way that it is interesting that there is no blood to be seen in the violent climax. This could be interpreted as part of the distanciation, a way of making us understand what is happening rather than reacting emotionally to it.

The Headmaster gives the boys a last chance, the privilege of service. They clear out junk, burn a stuffed alligator then, joined by the girl, discover a pickled foetus in a padlocked cupboard and a forgotten stack of arms under the school stage. 'One doesn't want to insist on the symbolism because that makes it sound clodhopping,' says Anderson of the foetus scene. 'First of all, it's got to work just as an incident under the stage. If you think of it also as a poetic symbol, the baby symbolises or

Stills: left – Bobby Philips, Wallace and Johnny. Above – Rowntree watches the distinguished guests arriving for Speech Day.

evokes life. But this is a life that is dead. It's been bottled up and deformed and therefore in that respect it also corresponds presumably to the flags, the boards, the lists of names and the books, all of which are also dead and discarded and shut away, have become just lumber; there's no longer any vitality in them. And presumably this could be said to relate to a tradition that no longer has any vitality and, if you like, is a tradition that is cutting off the springs of vitality, genuine vitality in the boys who are subjected to it. The three most lively and independent boys are beaten for their attitudes. So that relates presumably to this, that the girl appears and that it is actually with her that they go through beyond this cupboard in which are these images of death, and they find a heap of weapons, which in fact they later use. I would think that immediately there is an equation made between something which is the opposite of death, which is life, violence and sex.' (It should be added that Anderson

offers this kind of interpretation always with a show of reluctance, arguing that any other interpretation is likely to be equally valid.)

On Speech Day the platform party literally caricatures the tradition that no longer has any vitality (recalling for instance the people turned to dummies in *The White Bus*). Standing in front of two knights in medieval armour and a bishop in full regalia (church and army again), the Headmaster points out that 'there can be few places where tradition is examined with such a critical eye as this College,' and introduces the guest of honour, Denson's father, General Denson, Old Boy and national hero. 'Freedom is the heritage of every Englishman who speaks with the tongue that Shakespeare spoke,' says the General.' 'But we won't stay free, unless we're ready to fight.' And while he continues to talk fluently along these lines, the place goes up in smoke.

Boys and parents escape from the hall to be shot down in the quadrangle. 'Trust me,' says the well-meaning, reasonable Headmaster, and the girl shoots him from the roof. (Of course, it had to be the girl who did it; she stands most clearly for everything the system is suppressing.) The establishment counter-attacks. Mick is fighting with his back against the wall. One of the most liberating sequences that has ever appeared in a film, this is also defeat. *If . . .*, as Anderson has said, 'is like the writing on the wall.' The conflict of idealism – the necessity for it and its impossibility – is always present between people and between generations. It is a fighting for life.

If . . . is shot with a simplicity and control that finally stands above the more superficial discipline that is part of what it shows. Camera movements are usually unobtrusive, so that the long tracking and panning shots before and after the café scene (Mick's brief hour of freedom) carry an exceptional emotional charge.

Stills: the revolution. Chaos inside the hall; the establishment counter-attacks.

Describing the film as 'deeply anarchistic', Anderson has said that 'people persistently misunderstand the term anarchistic, and think it just means wildly chucking bombs about. But anarchy is a social and political philosophy which puts the highest possible value on responsibility. The film is not about responsibility against irresponsibility. It's about rival notions of responsibility and consequently well within a strong puritan tradition.'

The moral attitude of the film is evident in the order that Anderson has imposed on everything, and particularly on scenes of emotional release: the beauty of the gymnasium love scene with Wallace and Bobby Philips; the marvellous panning shot away from the café with the girl's hair flowing outwards as she rides erect behind her two companions on the motor bike, to the challenging and liberating music of the Missa Luba; the magnificently cut closing sequence. Moments like these, that express emotion with the discipline of art, are finally what the film stands for.

'Stylistically,' says Anderson, 'I don't really think *If . . .* fits very closely into a contemporary picture of film-making, except in so far as developments in the last – what? – ten years have made it possible to work with much greater freedom in the cinema than before, and to be personal and not to be bound to the traditional and conventional ideas of narrative construction and narrative style.

'I think where it isn't contemporary is that its technique I would say on the whole is extremely sober. In fact, this is both natural to me and the result of a quite conscious determination on my part. The more what we might call "trendy" or eccentric or showy, technique has tended to become in the last few years, the

more I have felt I wanted to try and make films with as much simplicity and as much directness as possible. Of course, simplicity and directness are actually the most difficult things, and sometimes one fails to bring it off maybe and is simply dull. But this is the direction in which I try to work. I'm quite out of sympathy with the modern school of criticism which says that you should just let things happen in front of the camera, and then the audience creates the film for themselves. I don't believe in letting the audience create the film. I feel that it's my job to create the film, my prerogative as an artist. Qualities of rhythm and balance and composition inside a very straightforward and sober technique are the problems that interest me most.

'In fact, the film has very little to do with current fashion either in terms of morality, i.e. the permissive society, or in terms of art and style. One of the things that I was very concerned to avoid when we were starting to make the film and planning the design of the film was any suggestion of what is currently known as "trendy", which would be terribly easy when you're dealing with a film about young people. So that we haven't used any of the kind of contemporarily fashionable allusions or tags that would be used in a trendy film about young people made for the permissive society. We've very deliberately avoided specific references of this kind.'

All this is recognisably an attitude and a way of working that Anderson has always held. The difference between If . . . and his earlier films is in having a subject that has finally enabled him to prove the validity of the Free Cinema credo that 'no film can be too personal'. It is because he can show this school environment with the ruthlessness and humour of one who has survived it and yet bears the marks of it,

that his film extends so naturally beyond realism into metaphor. He has succeeded best in the Free Cinema aim to show the significance of the everyday, by concentrating not on what is ordinary to other people but on what is ordinary to himself, on that authentic, upper middle-class background where, presumably, all his conflicts began.

All the ambiguities are contained in the characterisation, and the casting, of Malcolm McDowell as the hero. He is, says Anderson, 'a hero in the good, honourable, old-fashioned sense of the word. He is someone who arrives at his own beliefs, and stands up for those beliefs, if necessary against the world.' Yet what he is fighting is the denial of the heart inherent in the system, the same denial of the heart that turns him into a monster. And so he has no soft edges, makes no demands for sympathy. He is an absolutely unsentimental figure in whom it is possible to see society's impression of youthful delinquency as well as its traditional opposition to the kind of intransigence that characterises non-conformists. Unaccepting and unacceptable, he stands defiantly against the values to which the majority subscribe. There are no illusions in If . . .

'Every good writer,' wrote Cyril Connolly, with whose criticism Anderson's has rightly been compared, 'must discover the yawning crevasse which separates Man's finite destiny from his infinite potentialities. It is afterwards that he will reveal his artistic courage and so register the protest which is a final plea for order, his "Gulliver's Travels", his "Maxims", his "Songs of Experience", his "Saison en Enfer", his "Fleurs du Mal". The rest either pretend that they have seen nothing, and that all is well, or else howl with self-pity.'

This is what being uncompromising really means, and few film-makers have measured up to it. Anderson, in making If . . . , became one of them.

Still: the revolutionaries.

Filmography

Born 1923 in Bangalore, South India, where his Scots father was serving as an officer in the Royal Engineers. Had come to England by the time he was two. Educated at South Coast preparatory school and Cheltenham College, where he ended up as Head of his House for a term. Went up to Wadham College, Oxford, as classics scholar before being commissioned into the 60th Rifles and then attached to the Intelligence Corps during the war, the last year of which was spent in India working on cryptography. Returned to Oxford to take degree in English; wrote for 'Isis' and was co-founder, editor and regular contributor to 'Sequence'. Author of book 'Making A Film' and producer and actor in James Broughton's film *The Pleasure Garden* (1952). Organised season of John Ford's films at the National Film Theatre (1955). Supervising editor on Lorenza Mazzetti's *Together* (1956) and the documentary *March To Aldermaston* (1958). Originating member of Free Cinema (1956–59). Has written many articles and reviews for 'Sight and Sound', 'The Times', 'Observer', 'New Statesman', 'Encore'. Works mainly as a theatre director in the (usually long) gaps between films, and makes television commercials. Appears as an actor from time to time. Was appointed a Governor of the British Film Institute in 1969.

Films

1948: MEET THE PIONEERS. Richard Sutcliffe Ltd. Directed by Lindsay Anderson. Produced by Desmond and Lois Sutcliffe. Photographed by John Jones and Edward Brendon. Edited by Lindsay Anderson and Edward Brendon. Art adviser: Eric Westbrook. Music arranged by Len Scott. Commentary spoken by Lindsay Anderson. 33 minutes.

1949: IDLERS THAT WORK. Richard Sutcliffe Ltd. Directed by Lindsay Anderson. Produced by Richard O'Brien. Photographed by George Levy. Music from Ralph Vaughan Williams and Aaron Copland. Con-tinuity: Lois Sutcliffe. Unit assistants: Bill Longley, Geoff Oakes, Ernest Slinger and George Wilby. Commentary spoken by Lindsay Anderson. 17 minutes.

1952: THREE INSTALLATIONS. Richard Sutcliffe Ltd. Directed by Lindsay Anderson. Produced by Dermod Sutcliffe. Photographed by Walter Lassally. Additional photography by John Jones. Assistant cameraman: Desmond Davis. Edited by Derek York. Orchestral music from Copland, Gillis and Khatchachurian; Conveyor Boogie by Alan Clare (piano) and Johnny Flanagan (drums). Sound recording by Charles Green. Production manager: John Exley. Unit assistant: Vincent Young. Commentary spoken by Lindsay Anderson. 28 minutes.

1952: WAKEFIELD EXPRESS. The Wakefield Express Series Ltd. Directed by Lindsay Anderson. Produced by Michael Robinson. Photographed by Walter Lassally. Songs by Snapethorpe and Horbury Secondary Modern Schools; Band Music by Horbury Victoria Prize Band. Production assistant: John Fletcher. Commentary spoken by George Potts. 33 minutes.

1953: THURSDAY'S CHILDREN. World Wide Pictures (A Morse Production). Written and directed by Guy Brenton and Lindsay Anderson. Photographed by Walter Lassally. Music by Geoffrey Wright. Commentary spoken by Richard Burton. With children from the Royal School for the Deaf, Margate. 20 minutes.

1953: O DREAMLAND. A Sequence Film. Directed by Lindsay Anderson. Camera and assistance: John Fletcher. 12 minutes.

1954: TRUNK CONVEYOR. Richard Sutcliffe Ltd./ National Coal Board.
Directed by Lindsay Anderson. Produced by Dermod Sutcliffe. Photographed by John Reid. Camera assistant: Gerry Godfrey. Edited by Bill Megarry. Assistant editor: James Vans Collina. Songs by Bert Lloyd; Concertina, Alf Edwards; Guitar, Fitzroy Coleman. Production manager: Peter Woodward. Commentary spoken by Lindsay Anderson. 38 minutes.

1955: GREEN AND PLEASANT LAND.
HENRY.
THE CHILDREN UPSTAIRS.
A HUNDRED THOUSAND CHILDREN.
National Society for the Prevention of Cruelty to Children. (Basic Film Productions).
Directed and scripted by Lindsay Anderson. Produced by Leon Clore. Photographed by Walter Lassally. *Henry* 5½ minutes; the others each 4 minutes.

1955: £20 A TON.
ENERGY FIRST. National Industrial Fuel Efficiency Service. (Basic Film Productions).
Directed by Lindsay Anderson. Produced by Leon Clore. Photographed by Larry Pizer. Production manager: John Fletcher. Each about 5 minutes.

1955: FOOT AND MOUTH. Central Office of Information for the Ministry of Agriculture, Fisheries and Food (A Basic Film Production).
Written and directed by Lindsay Anderson. Produced by Leon Clore. Photographed by Walter Lassally. Edited by Bill Megarry. Technical adviser: J. C. Davidson, M.R.C.V.S. Production manager: Philip Aizlewood. Commentary spoken by Lindsay Anderson. 20 minutes.

1957: EVERY DAY EXCEPT CHRISTMAS. Ford of Britain (A Graphic Production).
Directed by Lindsay Anderson. Produced by Leon Clore and Karel Reisz. Photographed by Walter Lassally. Music by Daniel Paris. Recording and sound editing by John Fletcher. Assistants: Alex Jacobs, Brian Probyn and Maurice Ammar. Commentary spoken by Alun Owen. 40 minutes.

1963: THIS SPORTING LIFE. Independent Artists (A Julian Wintle/Leslie Parkyn Production).
Directed by Lindsay Anderson. Produced by Karel Reisz. Screenplay by David Storey, based on his novel 'This Sporting Life'. Photographed by Denys Coop. Camera operator: John Harris. Edited by Peter Taylor. Assistant editor: Tom Priestley. Art director: Alan Withy. Set dresser: Peter Lamont. Dress designer: Sophie Devine. Music composed by Roberto Gerhard

and conducted by Jacques-Louis Monod. Sound editor: Chris Greenham. Sound recording: John W. Mitchell and Gordon K. McCallum. Casting: Miriam Brickman. In charge of production: Albert Fennell. Assistant director: Ted Sturgis. Production manager: Geoffrey Haine. Continuity: Pamela Mann. Make-up: Bob Lawrence. Hairdresser: Ivy Emmerton. Propertyman: Ernie Quick. 134 minutes.
With Richard Harris (Frank Machin), Rachel Roberts (Mrs Hammond), Alan Badel (Weaver), William Hartnell (Johnson), Colin Blakely (Maurice Braithwaite), Vanda Godsell (Mrs Weaver), Arthur Lowe (Slomer), Anne Cunningham (Judith), Jack Watson (Len Miller), Harry Markham (Wade), George Sewell (Jeff), Leonard Rossiter (Phillips), Frank Windsor (Dentist), Peter Dugoid (Doctor), Wallas Eaton (Waiter), Anthony Woodruff (Head Waiter), Katherine Parr (Mrs Farrer), Bernadette Benson (Lynda), Andrew Nolan (Ian), Michael Logan (Riley), Murray Evans (Hooker), Tom Clegg (Gower), John Gill (Cameron), Ken Traill (Trainer).

1966: THE WHITE BUS. United Artists (A Woodfall Film Presentation).
Directed by Lindsay Anderson. Executive producer: Oscar Lewenstein. Associate producer: Michael Deeley. Original story and screenplay by Shelagh Delaney. Photographed by Miroslav Ondricek in black and white and colour. Edited by Kevin Brownlow. Art director: David Marshall. Music by Misha Donat. Sound editor: John Fletcher. Sound recording: Peter Handford. Casting director: Miriam Brickman. Assistant director: Kip Gowans. Production manager: Jake Wright. 46 minutes.
With Patricia Healey (The Girl), Arthur Lowe (The Mayor), John Sharp (The Macebearer), Julie Perry (Bus Conductress), Victor Henry ('Transistorite'), Stephen Moore (Smart Young Man), Fanny Carby (Football Supporter), Anthony Hopkins (Brechtian Singer), Jeanne Watts (Fish and Chip Shop Woman), Alaba Peters, Ronald Lacey and Margaret Barron.

1967: RAZ DWA TRZY – THE SINGING LESSON. Contemporary Films (Warsaw Documentary Studios.)
Directed by Lindsay Anderson. Chief of production: Miroslaw Podolski. Photographed by Zygmunt Samosiuk. Edited by Barbara Kosidowska. Arrangement of songs: Ludwik Sempolinski. Piano accompaniment: Irena Klukowna. Sound editor: Henryk Kuzniak. Sound recording: Malgorzata Jaworska. Assistant director: Joanna Nawrocka. 20 minutes.
Singers: Piotr Fronczewski ('The Coat'), Anita Przysiecka and Marian Glinka ('Big Beat'), Aniceta Raczek ('A Lullaby – for those who wait'), Waldemar Walisiak

('Sunshine Street'), Andrzej Nardelli ('Sweet Peas'), Joanna Sobieska and Andrzej Seweryn ('Oh, Miss Sabina!').

1968: IF . . . Paramount (A Memorial Enterprises Film). Directed by Lindsay Anderson. Produced by Michael Medwin and Lindsay Anderson. Screenplay by David Sherwin, from the original script 'Crusaders' by David Sherwin and John Howlett. Director of photography (in colour and black and white): Miroslav Ondricek. Cameraman: Chris Menges. Camera operator: Brian Harris. Camera assistant: Michael Seresin. Edited by David Gladwell. Assistant editors: Ian Rakoff and Michael Ellis. Production designed by Jocelyn Herbert. Wardrobe: Shura Cohen. Music composed and conducted by Marc Wilkinson; 'Sanctus' from the 'Missa Luba' (Philips recording). Dubbing editor: Alan Bell. Dubbing mixer: Doug Turner. Sound recordist: Christian Wangler. Casting director: Miriam Brickman. Assistant director: John Stoneman. Production manager: Gavrik Losey. Assistant to the producers: Neville Thompson. Assistants to the director: Stephen Frears and Stuart Baird. Continuity: Valerie Booth. Make-up: Betty Blattner. Construction manager: Jack Carter. 112 minutes.
With: *Crusaders* – Malcolm McDowell (Mick), David Wood (Johnny), Richard Warwick (Wallace), Christine Noonan (The Girl), Rupert Webster (Bobby Philips); *Whips* – Robert Swann (Rowntree), Hugh Thomas (Denson), Michael Cadman (Fortinbras), Peter Sproule (Barnes); *Staff* – Peter Jeffrey (Headmaster), Arthur Lowe (Mr Kemp), Mona Washbourne (Matron), Mary MacLeod (Mrs Kemp), Geoffrey Chater (Chaplain), Ben Aris (John Thomas), Graham Crowden (History Master), Charles Lloyd Pack (Classics Master), Anthony Nicholls (General Denson), Tommy Godfrey (Finchley); *Seniors* – Guy Ross (Stephans), Robin Askwith (Keating), Richard Everett (Pussy Graves), Philip Bagenal (Peanuts), Nicholas Page (Cox), Robert Yetzes (Fisher), David Griffin (Willens), Graham Sharman (Van Eyssen), Richard Tombleson (Baird); *Juniors* – Richard Davis (Machin), Brian Pettifer (Biles), Michael Newport (Brunning), Charles Sturridge (Markland), Sean Bury (Jute), Martin Beaumont (Hunter).

Theatre productions
1957: 'The Waiting of Lester Abbs' by Kathleen Sully at the Royal Court Theatre (30 June). Directed by Lindsay Anderson. A Sunday night production without décor. With Ian Bannen (Lester Abbs), Gladys Spencer (Sarah Abbs), Catherine Wilmer (Lilian Abbs), Mary Manson (Mary Pinham), Anthony Creighton (Melton), Geoffrey Belman (Barnes), Peter Bennett (Walton),

Alfred Burke (The Figure), Michael Wynne (Williams and Policeman), Anna Steele (Cynthia Totten), Alun Owen (Smith), Claire Pollock (Barmaid), Amos Brandstatter (Man at bar and C.I.D. man), Alistair Speed (Young man), Brigid Panet (Girl), Fanny Carby (Pat), Gerald Blake (Mr Brown and Warder), James Beatty (Bert), Barbara Hicks (Mrs Brown), Angela Crowe (Nellie), Michael Hastings (Alfie), Robert Hollyman (Landlord and Warder), John Dexter (C.I.D. Sgt. and Chaplain), Robert Stephens (Warder).

1959: 'The Long and the Short and the Tall' by Willis Hall at the Royal Court Theatre (7 January), transferred to the New Theatre (8 April). Directed by Lindsay Anderson. Décor by Alan Tagg. With Peter O'Toole (877 Pte. Bamforth, C.), Robert Shaw (465 Sgt. Mitchem, R.), Edward Judd (839 Cpl. Johnstone, E.), Ronald Fraser (594 L/Cpl. Macleish, A.J.), David Andrews (632 Pte. Whitaker, S.), Alfred Lynch (777 Pte. Evans, T.E.), Bryan Pringle (611 Pte. Smith, P.), Kenji Takaki (Japanese Soldier).

1959: 'Progress to the Park' by Alun Owen at the Royal Court Theatre (8 February). Directed by Lindsay Anderson. A Sunday night production without décor. With Harry H. Corbett (The Young Man), Tom Bell (Bobby Laughlin), Margaret Tyzack (Mag Keegan), Gerard Dynevor (Captain Laughlin), Bee Duffell (Mrs Laughlin), Donal Donnelly (Pat Jamieson), Keith Smith (Charlie Modryb), Joyce Latham (Mrs Keegan), Fanny Carby (Mrs Jones), Donald Howarth (Salvation Army Captain), Harry Gwyn-Davis (Captain Shinge).

1959: 'Serjeant Musgrave's Dance' by John Arden at the Royal Court Theatre (22 October). Directed by Lindsay Anderson. Décor by Jocelyn Herbert. Music by Dudley Moore. With Ian Bannen (Serjeant Musgrave), Donal Donnelly (Private Sparky), Alan Dobie (Private Hurst), Frank Finlay (Private Attercliffe), James Bree (Bludgeon), Richard Caldicot (The Parson), Freda Jackson (Mrs Hitchcock), Patsy Byrne (Annie), Michael Hunt (The Constable), Stratford Johns (The Mayor), Jack Smethurst (A Slow Collier), Colin Blakely (A Pugnacious Collier), Harry Gwynn Davies (Walsh), Barry Wilsher (A Trooper of Dragoons), Clinton Greyn (An Officer of Dragoons).

1960: 'The Lily White Boys' by Harry Cookson with songs by Christopher Logue and music by Tony Kinsey and Bill Le Sage at the Royal Court Theatre (27 January). Directed by Lindsay Anderson. Décor by Sean Kenny. Musical numbers staged by Eleanor Fazan. With *The Boys* – Albert Finney (Ted), Monty Landis (Razzo), Philip Locke (Musclebound); *The Girls* – Georgia Brown

(Jeannie), Shirley Ann Field (Eth), Ann Lynn (Liz); *The Upright Citizens* – Willoughby Goddard (The Chairman of the Committee and The Managing Director), James Grout (Businessman, Head Waiter, First Working Man and Policeman), Geoffrey Hibbert (Solicitor, Factory Manager, 2nd Working Man and Psychiatrist), Barbara Hicks (The Lady Committee Member, Factory Overseer, Waitress, Miss Peaches and Policewoman Clark), Ronnie Stevens (Youth Leader, Split-it, TV Interviewer, Trades Council Secretary and Daddy's Boy).

1960: 'Billy Liar' by Keith Waterhouse and Willis Hall (adapted from the novel of the same name by Keith Waterhouse) at the Cambridge Theatre (13 September). Directed by Lindsay Anderson. Décor by Alan Tagg. With Albert Finney (Billy Fisher), George A. Cooper (Geoffrey Fisher), Mona Washbourne (Alice Fisher), Ethel Griffies (Florence Boothroyd), Trevor Bannister (Arthur Crabtree), Ann Beach (Barbara), Juliet Cooke (Rita), Jennifer Jayne (Liz).

1960: 'Trials by Logue': two one-act plays by Christopher Logue with music by Bill Le Sage at the Royal Court Theatre (23 November). Directed by Lindsay Anderson, Décor by Jocelyn Herbert. 'Antigone' with Mary Ure (Antigone), George Rose (Creon), Zoe Caldwell (Ismene), Morris Perry (Head Stewart), Trevor Martin (Second Stewart), Murray Evans (Third Stewart), Dickie Owen (Head Guard), Peter Fraser (Second Guard), Tony Selby (Third Guard), Peter Duguid (Sentry), Laurence Harrington (Fourth Guard), Peter Holmes (Haemon). 'Cob and Leach' with Mary Ure (Mabel Cob), Peter Fraser (Henry Leach), George Rose (Magistrate), Zoe Caldwell (Whore), Peter Duguid (Clerk of the Court), Morris Perry (First Policeman), Murray Evans (Second Policeman), Hazel Hughes (Miss Edith Peaches), Trevor Martin (Sergeant Pokesdown), Tony Selby and Dickie Owen (Police Horse Charlotte), Peter Holmes (Plato, a dog), Tony Stone (Policewoman Suet, bass), Brian Pickles (Constable Mogg, drums), Stanley Myers (Sergeant Posey, piano).

1961: 'The Fire Raisers' by Max Frisch (translated by Michael Bullock) at the Royal Court Theatre (21 December). Directed by Lindsay Anderson. Décor by Alan Tagg. Music by Dudley Moore. With Alfred Marks (Gottlieb Biedermann), Ann Beach (Anna), Colin Blakely (Schmitz), Doris Hare (Babette Biedermann), James Booth (Eisenring), Roger Kemp (Policeman and Fireman), Catherine Wilmer (Widow Knechtling), John Thaw (Doctor of Philosophy and Fireman), Norman Henry (Chief Fireman), Trevor Danby; David Jackson,

Dickie Owen, Gordon Rollings and Henry Woolf (Firemen). Preceded by a one-act curtain-raiser 'Box and Cox' by John Maddison Morton. With James Booth (Box), Colin Blakely (Cox), Doris Hare (Mrs Bouncer).

1963: 'The Diary of a Madman' adapted by Lindsay Anderson and Richard Harris from the story by Gogol, at the Royal Court Theatre (7 March). Directed by Lindsay Anderson. Décor by Voytek. With Richard Harris (Aksenti Ivanovitch).

1964: 'Andorra' by Max Frisch (translated by Michael Bullock) at the National Theatre (28 January). Directed by Lindsay Anderson. Décor by John Bury. Costumes by John Bury and Una Collins. With Tom Courtenay (Andri), Lynn Redgrave (Barblin), Colin Blakely (Peider), Diana Wynyard (The Senora), Trevor Martin (Innkeeper), James Mellor (Prader), Robert Stephens (Father Benedict), Robert Lang (Anyone), Cyril Cusack (Can), Michael Turner (Idiot), Derek Jacobi (Fedri), Anthony Nicholls (Ferrer), Wynne Clark (Mother), Peter Cellier (The Jew Detector).

1964: 'Julius Caesar' by William Shakespeare at the Royal Court Theatre (26 November). Directed by Lindsay Anderson. Décor by Jocelyn Herbert. Music by Marc Wilkinson. With Paul Curran (Julius Caesar), Ian Bannen (Brutus), Daniel Massey (Mark Antony), T. P. McKenna (Cassius), Graham Crowden (Casca), Nan Munro (Calpurnia), Sheila Allen (Portia), Peter Brett (Flavius and Messala), Rex Robinson (Marullus and Octavius' Captain), Nicholas Grimshaw (Cicero), David Jackson (Cinna), Robert McBain (Decius Brutus and Lepidus), Anthony Hopkins (Metullus Cimber), Lew Luton (Trebonius), Malcolm Reynolds (Lucius), Harry Hutchinson (Ligarius and A Poet), Douglas Ditta (Caesar's servant), Milton Johns (Artemidorus and Cinna the poet), Stephen Moore (Antony's servant and Titinius), Ronald Pickup (Octavius Caesar), John Dunn Hill (Strato), Henry Stamper (Pindarus), Edwin Finn (A Soothsayer).

1966: 'The Cherry Orchard' by Anton Chekhov at the Chichester Festival Theatre (July 19). Directed by Lindsay Anderson. Décor by Alan Tagg. Music by Misha Donat. Dances arranged by Eleanor Fazan. With Celia Johnson (Mme Ranyevskaia), Tom Courtenay (Trofimov), Sarah Badel (Ania), Zena Walker (Varia), Hugh Williams (Gayev), Ray McAnally (Lopakhin), Bill Fraser (Simeonov-Pishchik), Catherine Wilmer (Charlotta Ivanovna), John Standing (Yepihodov), Sheena Campbell (Dooniasha), John Laurie (Feers), Michael Burrell (Yasha), John Quarmby (A Tramp), Morris Jones (Station-Master), Gordon Reid (Post-

Office Clerk), Sheila Barker, Janet Hargreaves, Vivien Lloyd, Peter Egan, Ben Kingsley, Arthur Skinner (Guests and Servants).

1966: 'Inadmissible Evidence' by John Osborne at the Contemporary Theatre, Warsaw. Directed by Lindsay Anderson. With Tadeusz Lomnicki (Bill Maitland).

1969: 'In Celebration' by David Storey at the Royal Court Theatre (22 April). Directed by Lindsay Anderson. Décor by Peter Docherty. With Alan Bates (Andrew Shaw), Bill Owen (Mr Shaw), Constance Chapman (Mrs Shaw), James Bolam (Colin Shaw), Brian Cox (Steven Shaw), Gabrielle Daye (Mrs Burnett), Fulton Mackay (Reardon).

Television films

Episodes in 'The Adventures of Robin Hood' series. Incorporated Television Programme Company. (Weinstein Productions for Sapphire Films). Directed by Lindsay Anderson. Executive producer: Hannah Weinstein. Associate producer: Sidney Cole. Script supervisor: Albert G. Ruben. Photographed by Ken Hodges. Supervising editor: Thelma Connell. Art supervisor: William Kellner. Sound: H. C. Pearson. Assistant director: Christopher Noble. Production manager: Harold Buck. Each 25 minutes.

1955: 'Secret Mission'. Screenplay by Ralph Smart. Music: Edwin Astley. With Richard Greene (Robin Hood), Patrick Barr (Peregrinus), Alan Wheatley (Sheriff), Alexander Guage (Friar Tuck), Archie Duncan (Little John), John Longden (Wulfric), Charles Stapley (Will), Paul Connell (Innkeeper), Victor Woolf (Derwent).

1956: 'The Imposters'. Screenplay by Norman Best. Music: Edwin Astley. With Richard Greene (Robin Hood), Alexander Guage (Friar Tuck), Bernadette O'Farrell (Maid Marian), Archie Duncan (Little John), Brenda de Banzie (Lady Pomfret), Nigel Green (Prival), Jack Melford (Lord Pomfret), Edward Mulhare (Le Blond), Victor Woolf (Notarius), Paul Hansard (Rolf), Shaun O'Riordan (Quentin), Martin Lane (Tom).

1956: 'Ambush'. Screenplay by Ernest Borneman and Ralph Smart. Music: Albert Elms. With Richard Greene (Robin Hood), Alexander Guage (Friar Tuck), Bernadette O'Farrell (Maid Marian), Archie Duncan (Little John), Alan Wheatley (Sheriff), Donald Pleasence (Prince John), Peter Asher (Prince Arthur), Dorothy Alison (Constance), Victor Woolf (Derwent), Peter Bennett (Edwin), Shaun O'Riordan (Prince John's Captain), Edward Mulhare (Courtier), Martin Lane (Spy).

1956: 'The Haunted Mill'. Screenplay by Paul Symonds. Music: Edwin Astley. With Richard Greene (Robin Hood), Alexander Guage (Friar Tuck), Bernadette O'Farrell (Maid Marian), Alan Wheatley (Sheriff), Archie Duncan (Little John), James Hayter (Tom the Miller), Laurence Hardy (Sir William), John Schlesinger (Hale), Victor Woolf (Abbot of Whitby), Edward Mulhare (Baron Mornay), Peter Bennett (Edward), Shaun O'Riordan (Seneschal), Martin Lane (Page).

1956: 'Isabella'. Screenplay by Neil R. Collins. Music: Edwin Astley. With Richard Greene (Robin Hood), Bernadette O'Farrell (Maid Marian), Archie Duncan (Little John), Zena Walker (Isabella), Helen Cherry (Avice), Donald Pleasence (Prince John), Alan Edwards (Pembroke), Martin Lane (Sir Damon), Howard Lang (Landlord), Shaun O'Riordan (Page), Peter Bennett (Tavern keeper), Noel Hood (Old woman), Lynette Mills (Chambermaid), Nicholas Brady (Will), Isobel Greig (Maid-in-waiting).

Principal articles

Sequence – 'Angles of Approach' (2, Winter 1947), 'A Possible Solution' (3, Spring 1948), 'Creative Elements' (5, Autumn 1948), 'British Cinema: the Descending Spiral' (7, Spring 1949), 'The Films of Alfred Hitchcock' (9, Autumn 1949), 'They Were Expendable and John Ford' (11, Summer 1950), 'The Director's Cinema?' (12, Autumn 1950), 'Goldwyn at Claridges' (Interview with Samuel Goldwyn. 13, New Year 1951), 'The Quiet Man' (Interview with John Ford. 14, New Year 1952).

Sight and Sound – 'Only Connect: Some Aspects of the Work of Humphrey Jennings' (April-June 1954), 'The Last Sequence of On The Waterfront' (January-March 1955), 'Stand Up! Stand Up!' (Autumn 1956), 'Notes from Sherwood' (Winter 1956–57), 'Ten Feet Tall' (Summer 1957), 'Two Inches Off The Ground' (Winter 1957–58).

Declaration (1957) – 'Get Out And Push!'

International Theatre Annual (No.5, 1961) – 'Pre-Renaissance'.

Films and Filming (February 1963) – 'Sport, Life and Art' (Anderson interviewed mainly about *This Sporting Life*).

Jeune Cinéma (39, May 1969) – Interview with Anderson (mainly about *If . . .*).